WINE BRANDS

Wine Brands

Success Strategies for New Markets, New Consumers and New Trends

Evelyne Resnick

palgrave
macmillan

First published in 2008 by
PALGRAVE MACMILLAN
Houndmills, Basingstoke, Hampshire RG21 6XS and
175 Fifth Avenue, New York, N.Y. 10010
Companies and representatives throughout the world.

PALGRAVE MACMILLAN is the global academic imprint of the Palgrave
Macmillan division of St. Martin's Press, LLC and of Palgrave Macmillan Ltd.
Macmillan® is a registered trademark in the United States, United Kingdom
and other countries. Palgrave is a registered trademark in the European
Union and other countries.

ISBN-13: 978–0–230–55403–0
ISBN-10: 0–230–55403–2

This book is printed on paper suitable for recycling and made from fully
managed and sustained forest sources. Logging, pulping and manufacturing
processes are expected to conform to the environmental regulations of
the country of origin.

A catalogue record for this book is available from the British Library.

A catalog record for this book is available from the Library of Congress.

10   9   8   7   6   5   4   3   2   1
17   16   15   14   13   12   11   10   09   08

Printed and bound in Great Britain by
Cromwell Press Ltd, Trowbridge, Wiltshire

To Joan Dillon, Duchesse de Mouchy
and her son, Prince Robert de Luxembourg.
Whose trust is an honor and an inspiration.

In loving memory of my father, Bertrand Lejeune
and my grand mother, Hélène Rochery de Marcenay.
Whose love for wine and food started my passion for
good living and excellence.

Contents

List of Illustrations

List of Tables

Acknowledgements

Writing a book puts the author in debt to so many people that it is difficult to know where to start, but it was a delight to call on people – known or unknown – or email them with questions and to get spontaneous and friendly answers from them. I was lucky and made happy to meet many wonderful people, to renew my acquaintance with people I had not had the opportunity of talking to for some time and to keep in touch with friends and colleagues.

First of all, I want to thank the wonderful woman who trusted my husband Randolph, myself and our small consulting firm with her web site and online communication, Joan Dillon, Duchess of Mouchy. Thanks to her continuing trust and now that of her son, Prince Robert of Luxembourg, we were introduced to the world of fine wines, and were able to get involved in the web communication and marketing of great wines. Their generosity, kindness and open-mindedness make working with them a pleasure and an inspiration to excellence. We feel very privileged to work with them.

Because we had the trust of Duchess de Mouchy and Prince Robert, other prestigious Bordeaux estates and wine properties all over France have given us their trust. I would like to thank Bertrand Bouteiller, former manager of Château Palmer, Bernard de Laage de Meux, Development Director, Thomas Duroux, current manager and their wonderful team for the many hours, and sometimes days, spent at the Château engaged in brainstormings, as well as meals accompanied by great Palmer vintages.

Of course, all our clients contribute to the joy of working which we feel everyday. Whether from Champagne, Burgundy, Provence or the South West, they all received us as friends and welcomed us as part of their team. This is the privilege of belonging to the world of fine wines filled by fine people.

Writing this book in English was an adventure and a challenge for me since English is not my first language. I had to call on my many English-speaking friends to help me. There are some friends whose email boxes were very often filled with requests and silly questions. A million thanks go to my dear friends, Don and Petie Kladstrup, whose talent as writers and vast knowledge of wine history were very often called upon. They had the patience to proofread all the chapters of this book, and their comments were always very valuable and much welcomed. They knew when to challenge me, and to ask questions which opened up new roads and new thoughts. They spent a lot of time on the phone listening to my doubts and comforting me when I thought my task was too difficult. A million thanks for their uncomplaining friendship and support.

Thanks also to Christopher Cartwright whose perfect command of English was such a help when grammar and spelling questions arose – quite often. His patience and kindness were invaluable.

This book was just a vague idea in my mind when I met Uche Okonkwo, founder of Luxe E.t.c. and author of *Luxury Fashion Brands*. Uche is certainly one of the most talented and bright young women I have met in my career. During a business meeting I mentioned to her casually that I was thinking of a book on wine and web marketing, since the subject had not been covered yet. She immediately told me to contact her publisher, and thanks to her kindness the project was accepted. There are no words to thank such a generous and kind person sufficiently.

Because of Uche I had the pleasure of meeting my editor, Alexandra Dawe, and working with her during the long months of writing. She answered all the queries and all the questions which an anguished writer has. Many thanks to her for her patience and kindness.

I should not forget to thank all the friends, colleagues and wine professionals who have answered my questions, gone out of their way to help me and were always patient with my requests: Hoke Harden, Kimberly Charles, Paul Wagner, Stuart Yaniger, Bernard Roth, who introduced me to the Mission grape, James de Roany and Jérémy Arnaud, just to mention a few.

Last but not least, my husband Randolph, whose patience must have sometimes been strained, when, for many months, the book took precedence over almost everything. He has also contributed a lot to this book by taking pictures, opening doors to people to interview and suggesting ideas on various subjects. He never complained during the writing and completion of this work, and I am so grateful for his kind understanding and total support.

Introduction

Once upon a time there was an aspiring writer in Paris, France … That is how my story and this story of wine brands started.

When I started writing professionally in 1975, I had to type my texts on a manual typewriter. I remember very clearly the evenings spent laboring over a keyboard so hard I had calluses on the tips of my fingers – let alone the damage caused to my nail polish. While working on my MA thesis a few years later, I happily graduated to an electric type-writer – so smooth it did not endanger my nail polish. But I still had to retype all the pages of my dissertation over and over each time I made changes.

In 1979, when I was completing my PhD, I had access, wonder of wonders, to a computer with a word processor! What a luxury! It is true I had by then moved to the United States, a country much more advanced technologically than Europe. It was such a pleasure to insert and suppress paragraphs, to move them around from one page to another, to correct typos and mistakes without redoing the same work over and over again. I was even able to manage a small database of literary opinions about women writers extracted from many books, and then analyze them using a program written by my husband. This 'scientific' way of analyzing literary texts was a little puzzling to my adjudicators, but interested them enough to award me my PhD with honors.

When I was teaching at UCLA and researching for my books and my classes, I spent hours in libraries taking notes by hand and then entering them into my computer. A second miracle happened when I was writing my first book: a portable computer. Of course, it was big and heavy. Of course, there was only one plug in a research room for portable computers. Of course, librarians and researchers thought I was a nuisance with the slight click of my keyboard and the purring of the computer. Of course, I still had to go to libraries and use snail mail or faxes to get in touch with colleagues and peers all over the world.

By the time I was working on my second book, a third miracle had occurred: the Internet was available. No more libraries, no more snail mail, no more faxes. Research on line and emails changed my life, my working habits and my way of thinking.

Why did I tell you my life story? Because it is a pattern reflected in many sectors of activity. What was happening in the early 1980s, with computers and word processors, is now happening in the business world with the new technologies. Computers, word processors and software changed our way of working, and even of thinking, very deeply. The Internet has changed, is changing and, more and more, will continue to change our ways of working, thinking and consuming. Young people born in the 1980s grew up with the technology, and cannot even imagine using a pen or a pencil, not to mention paper, for these tasks. They were raised with computers, Internet connections, MP3 players, mobile phones, TV on demand, Skype and Internet phones. Every industry is affected by what some call 'progress' and others call 'disaster.'

What is happening with the Internet happened with the wine industry. When I was a child in the 1960s, my parents drank a glass of wine with their dinner. I grew up thinking I would drink wine, preferably French, but life took me away from home and gave me the opportunity to taste wines from the 'New World' – California, Australia, Argentina, to name a few. I discovered a full range of tastes, colors, varieties and quality. I also learned that drinking wine with a meal was not always the custom, or even the proper thing to do. Bottom line, I was experiencing world culture before its time. Back in France, I saw a change in the drinking and eating habits of French people and of others all over Europe. Life was changing and so were the habits of consumers.

For a long time, indeed, wine was exclusively a field for men. Professionals and wine drinkers were mostly male, collecting great wines and drinking some wine with their meals every day. Most such wines came from Europe, even if some people knew that other countries produced wines. In 1976 a comparative tasting of American and French wines saw the victory of the Californians. The now famous 'Judgment of Paris' aroused the interest of some wine lovers and professionals in non-European wines. Australia, New Zealand, Chile and Argentina started producing wines and exporting them to the United States and the United Kingdom. The rise of an international wine industry changed the way of drinking for many people. Wine drinkers had more choice in style, quality, price and varieties. Wine drinkers changed too. Women and young people became interested in wine as it became more widely spread and available. Life also changed. More women went to work, food became 'fast food,' Starbucks' coffees became a lifestyle food. The industry had to adjust to these new behavioral patterns and sociological changes.

The conjunction of the rise of new technologies and new trends in producing and consuming wine gave birth to a new marketing approach for the rather conservative wine market. Marketing wine is not rocket science, but it has developed enough methodology over the last 20 years to be effective and to provide a return on investment. Web marketing, on the other hand, is a new discipline, and still has to prove its efficiency and its profitability. Winemakers and the trade did not yet recognize and acknowledge the importance of a Web strategy to promote and sell wines. That is what this book is about.

How can the virtual world of the Internet help to sell an agricultural and cultural product such as wine? There is no frontier in the virtual world. The most obscure winery located in the most secluded part of the most unknown country can access potential wine customers through the Internet. The winery does not even need a web site. A mention on a search engine or in a blog is enough for its name to pop up in front of the eyes of a wine drinker. Then word of mouth or viral marketing will give it more visibility.

How did the wine industry get to such a level of sophistication? The history of wine is one of culture, but also of misery and mediocrity. For centuries, Europe produced great wines from prestigious estates and mediocre wines from lesser properties. Whether wonderful or barely drinkable, however, all those wines were linked to their soil, their climate and the geography of the place. This distinction as a criteria of quality is still valid. Europe, America, Australia, Chile, Argentina and all the wine-producing countries sell high-quality and expensive wines alongside low quality and cheap wines (some not so cheap). But the link to the place grew weaker with the emergence of the new producing countries, which put the variety first.

Brand managers understood the customers' need for a simpler approach to wine culture. There is no need to know *terroir* and wine-making techniques to enjoy a wine. The language of wine also changed, and went from a technical approach to a more hedonistic perspective. The brand managers talked about taste, wine and food pairing and enjoyment, even when their wine got its qualities from a specific place or choice of winemaking method.

The language of wine changed because of, and along with, the new trends and new strategies invented by marketers and web marketers. 'Brand' does not need to be a dirty word if it covers a simple language rather than a simple wine. Of course – let us not be naïve – there were, are and will continue to be simple brands: remember Blue Nun, Vieux Papes or Paul Masson jug wines. Marketing and web marketing are about words and language, and that is also what blogs, forums, wikis and web sites are about.

Web 1.0 ..., Web 2.0 .... Now there is even talk about Web 3.0! The new technological tools made available by the Internet create new ways of talking about wine, its fascinating world and its evolution. It reaches everybody, the European traditional wine drinker, the American new drinker and the aspiring Indian wine drinker. Traditional and emerging markets, traditional and new drinkers, are the targets of a web site, a blog or a webcast.

History, tastes, colors, aromas – all the world of wine with its complexity, its controversies and its diversity is now available on the Web. The purpose of this book is to take readers through the history of wine in various countries, and to lead them into the twenty-first century, where wine is a new trend with new consumers and new markets.

Once upon a time a vine was planted ...

PART I

New and traditional consumers

CHAPTER 1

Portrait of a man as a traditional consumer

November 15, 2007, 12:01 AM, France. Millions of cases of *Beaujolais Nouveau* (the new Beaujolais wine, first of the year) are trucked out of a little French village to go across the world. In the United States, in the United Kingdom, in Japan, millions of wine drinkers are expecting the arrival of this easy-drinking wine and are ready to celebrate. All over the world, cafés, wine bars and restaurants have special evenings to enjoy the event and people rejoice – as a pre-Christmas celebration.

November 15, 2007, 3:00 AM, Idaho, USA. Ben, a young man in his early thirties, cannot get to sleep. He turns on his computer and starts surfing the Web. He logs onto the online store wine.com and buys a few bottles of wine and Champagne that he will share with his friends and family during the holidays.

November 15, 2007, 6:00 PM, Kyoto, Japan. Mariko, a young executive woman in her thirties, comes out of the office and meets her girlfriends in a wine bar. They all sip a glass of Beaujolais Nouveau rosé, the pink version of the new wine of the year, specially crafted for the Japanese market by the French winemakers. In Mumbai, India, in Beijing, China, and in Moscow, Russia, the Beaujolais Nouveau is not trendy enough to drive wine drinkers to wine bars while at the same hour, in Paris, France, older people are gathering in their local cafés (coffee shops) to spend the evening drinking the red Beaujolais Nouveau and eating sausage as they do all over France.

This instant picture of wine drinking all over the world depicts what happens in the first years of the New Millennium when the Internet changed our ways of working, living and consuming. But it had taken centuries for wine lovers to become so sophisticated and start behaving in a very similar way. For several centuries, the behavior of the consumer differed from one country to another. Wine and food were the reflections of the culture of every country for many years. To understand how wine became the expression of a universal culture it is necessary to go back in time and see how local tradition evolved to a universal culture.

Traditional markets

Europe, the United States and Japan have been considered traditional markets for wine since the end of World War II. By 'traditional' markets we mean countries open to imported foreign wines, like Japan, since the end of World War II. They expanded and developed in very different ways due to their cultural differences.

In Europe the history of wine is very old and has shaped the culinary habits of every country. It would be very difficult in a book focused on marketing to draw a complete picture of culinary and drinking habits in every country. We will focus on France, representative of the evolution of the European wine-producing countries that all sustained the same changes.

France, a long tradition of wine making

In France, monks were creating vineyards in Burgundy, whilst aristocrats were tending their properties in Bordeaux and Champagne from the Middle Ages right up to the French Revolution in 1789, at which time there were 100,000 taverns in France serving cheap wine. By then, indeed, there was wine for the rich and wine for the poor. The latter – city workers, peasants, laborers – were drinking a strong wine, supposedly to give them strength and energy for their hard day at work. The rich drank the delicate wines produced by the great vineyards of Burgundy, Bordeaux or Champagne.

The Revolutionary armies, and later the Imperial armies commanded by Napoleon Bonaparte, generated the need for a lot of wine. Producers and growers pooled their resources to produce large quantities of cheap wine to 'feed' millions of soldiers. At the same time, generals and the family of Bonaparte 'freed' the invaded countries from their monarchies and simultaneously, brought back to France some of their best wines, such as 30 barrels of Montalcino, together with some of the most beautiful paintings by Veronese! Simultaneously the confiscation of the vineyards owned by the monks and the aristocrats allowed very small owners to produce a cheap and easy to sell wine on the best lands.

During the years 1830–50, the development of the railway facilitated the delivery of wines from the producing regions to the major cities, and from the 1960s wine consumption increased all over France. During the nineteenth century two factors contributed to the development of a drinking problem in Europe. Transportation became a lot easier after the development of the train and rail freight as well as river traffic, and later on the price of wine went down dramatically because of oïdium and phylloxera problems, two diseases deadly to vines.

The urban middle-class as well as upper middle-class families now had a cellar, which included wines, spirits, beers and ciders. Its role was more for indicating social status than for enjoyment. For everyday drinking the middle-class family would serve a mediocre wine to which some water was added. At the same time the employees of the house – the maid, the cook and the servant – received 3 liters of wine a week for a man and 2 liters a week for a woman as part of their salary. In the country the laborer received about 2 liters *a day* from his employer as part of his salary. All these factors explain why wine consumption doubled between 1830 and the end of the nineteenth century.

Champagne, kings and sovereigns

During the Second Empire (1851–70), Napoleon III encouraged exports. Thanks to these new clients, the style of the wines became more diversified and the quality improved. The best example of the different taste is Champagne, as shown by Don and Petie Kladstrup in their recent *Champagne: How the World's Most Glamorous Wine Triumphed over War and Hard Times*. The Kladstrups discovered the book of an American visitor to Champagne, Robert Tomes, whose keen analysis of the market at that time is a precious testimony about the tastes of Champagne drinkers. He enjoyed tremendously the dryer taste of the Champagne, so different to the Champagne he had drunk in New York with his friends: 'It was the first time in my life that I had enjoyed a glass of Champagne, as wine. I now found, instead of tossing off my glass and swallowing its contents with a gulp, as I had been wont to do in order to secure the evanescent sparkle and hasten the expected exhilaration, that the wine trickled slowly, drop by drop, over the gratified palate.'[1]

Ready to go back to America, Tomes encouraged Champagne producers to be more sensitive to the palate of foreign consumers who, by then, represented 80 percent of the market. The Kladstrups summon up very clearly the state of the Champagne industry in 1867 when Tomes left France to return to America:

> In what constituted a farewell note, he accused producers of catering to 'the gulping crowd,' of making champagnes that all taste as if they were 'brewed from the same vat.' He leveled some specific criticisms. Heidsieck's

champagne, he said, 'no longer pleases the taste of the fastidious.' Though 'wholesome and pure,' it is 'too sweet for a discriminating palate.' Roederer's is 'loaded with sugar,' while Moët & Chandon is 'manufactured for the masses' and not admired by European connoisseurs.[2]

The legacy of Robert Tomes to the Champagne industry was not lost, since the Champagne houses, with France conquered by the Prussians in 1870 and with the consequences of America divided by the Civil War, are developing new markets. Louise Pommery was the leading figure in making dry Champagnes specifically for the British market. It was quite a gamble because making dry Champagne required better grapes and longer ageing in cellars (three years instead of one), increasing the financial costs. 'But the biggest risk,' explained the Kladstrups, 'was that most people knew only sweet Champagne and liked it that way. There were hints that customers might prefer something else if it were available. But they didn't come from France, they came from Britain, Pommery's main market.'[3]

Britain was overflowing with sweet wines: port, sherry and others. Its palate was ready for a change – why not a change initiated by the Champagne industry?

Louise Pommery had a very hard time creating her first dry Champagne. For three years after the Franco-Prussian war, weather was bad and the grapes of poor quality. In 1874, at last, a vintage heralded as the best of the century allowed Louise to make a Champagne so good that an ode was written to celebrate it:

> Farewell, then, Pommery Seventy-Four!
> With reverential sips
> We part and grieve that nevermore
> Such wine may pass our lips.

The very high quality of this vintage allowed the finance manager, Henri Vanier, to tell his clients: 'Our brut is meant only for people who appreciate fine sparkling drinks, who prefer finesse and bouquet to an excess of gas and sugar which some houses use to cover up the thinness of their wines. When the cork pops, our champagne will satisfy the palate, not just the ears.'[4]

Is it the success of Louise Pommery which encouraged the other Champagne makers to change their politics, listen to their customers and take care of their tastes? Whatever the reasons, another Champagne house, Roederer, catered to the very special needs of Czar Alexander II. The links between Champagne and the Russian court go back to the days of Peter the Great in the eighteenth century. Peter did not merely drink – he guzzled. 'So much so,' write the Kladstrups, 'that he passed out in a drunken stupor in the *crayères* that today belong to Taittinger Champagne; because Peter was so enormous, there was no alternative but to leave him where he'd collapsed until he came to.' In fact Peter 'made it a nightly habit to always go to bed with at least four bottles of champagne tucked in with him.'[5]

Champagne Roederer was the very favorite wine of the Russian Imperial family and especially of Czar Alexander II. In 1855 he announced that he preferred 'Roederer's intensely sweet style to all others … By 1868 two million bottles, or 80 percent of Roederer's annual worldwide sales, were going to Russia.'[6]

Alexander's passion for Roederer went even further. He sent his cellar master to Reims every year to select the best *cuvées* for his table. But fearful of being poisoned, he wanted his cellar master to control every step. He also demanded a bottle specially designed for him, instead of the dark green bottle usually provided. Roederer designed a clear and elegant crystal bottle, and accordingly named the Champagne 'Cristal': Cristal of Roederer was born!

From a drink every day to a drink every … ?

If the upper middle class and the rich could afford these new and elegant wines, the working man and his family had to rely on cheap, and very often adulterated, wines and alcoholic beverages. This sad situation did not reduce consumption (see Table 1.1). During World War I, the 1930s recession and World War II, wine and alcohol became the refuge of soldiers and the poor. The inferior quality of the products prompted professional winemakers to create the AOC system (Appellation d'origine controlée) in 1935 to control the quality of the wines.

The French wine industry was dying when in 1959 a miracle occured: a great and abundant vintage. Vintners were once again proud of their work and consumers were happy with their glass of wine.

While all these legal and economic changes were occurring, the tastes of consumers were changing in France as well as in the rest of Europe. Wine was still part of the meal, thanks to brands like 'Vieux Papes' launched in 1930. Modestly priced but decent-tasting Vieux Papes red wines are still sold today. They were on the table of almost every Frenchman in the 1960s and 1970s. By the 1980s French wine consumption had started to decline: Consumers were getting more discriminating, and, instead of a bottle of Vieux Papes every day, they switched to better quality wines once a week, or perhaps two or three times a month.

Table 1.1 Consumption of alcoholic beverages in France
from 1831 to 2000 (average by liter per inhabitant)

Date	Wine	Beer	Spirits
1831–34	86	9.4	1.23
1835/39	83	11.5	1.41
1840/44	80	12.0	1.75
1845/49	76	12.0	1.83
1850/54	76	12.8	1.78
1855/59	83	18.1	2.25
1860/64	107	18.6	2.36
1865/69	148	19.7	2.58
1870/74	136	19.8	2.57
1875/79	147	21.1	2.99
1880/84	104	23.4	3.95
1885/89	93	21.8	3.91
1890/94	108	22.3	4.42
1895/99	122	25.0	4.53
1900/04	168	27.7	4.0
1905/09	157	29.0	3.90
1910/13	128	32.9	4.22
1919/21	148	20.7	2.09
1922/24	194	29.4	3.25

Source: From Didier Nourrisson, *Le buveur au XIXe siècle*, p. 321.

The United States: a love-hate relationship with wine and food

The story of wine in America is in marked contrast, however. The relationship between alcohol and the American citizen is very different. Torn between prohibitionist tendencies and a taste for their good wines, Americans have a difficult time finding a balance between moderate wine consumption and cries of alcoholism. That is why wine consumption still faces ideological and legal impediments.

The Mission grape: the Heritage grape of California

The first immigrants coming from wine producing countries tried to introduce vineyards in their new country with varying success. Spanish missionaries were among the first to introduce wine production to California for the Mass as early as the seventeenth century. The local varieties (Scuppermong in Florida or Mission in California) gave mediocre juices – mostly suitable for Mass. In California, the story of wine is very much linked to the history of the missions. The Spanish priest Junipero Serra founded the first nine missions in California, and was about to start the foundation of the tenth in Santa Barbara in 1782 when he died. His successor, Father Fermin Francisco de Lasuen, raised the cross in front of what would be the future mission, and put Father Antonio Paterna, a companion of Serra, in charge. The Santa Barbara Mission was completed in 1786 (see Figure 1.1).

Their priests and their converts, the local Chumash Indians, were supposed to be self-sustaining. The priests introduced the Chumash to the cultivation of wheat, barley, corn, beans and peas. Orange and olive trees were planted, and vines were grown. Water was brought from the mountains creeks to irrigate the fields and for domestic use.

The vines planted by the priests were, logically, called 'Mission grape.' By now, 300 years after the mission building began, the original grapes are dead. But thanks to a woman in Santa Rita Hills, near Santa Barbara, 100 year-old Mission grapes are still alive and give some wine every year.

Figure 1.1   Santa Barbara Mission
Source: Photo by Resmo.

Deborah Hall (see Figure 1.2) bought Gypsy Canyon Winery with her late husband in 1994. On their land was a vast area covered with sage bush. It took a little while to clear up the area and, this done, Deborah saw vines. At first she thought it was Zinfandel and for two years sold her grapes to

Figure 1.2   Deborah Hall in her barn at Gypsy Canyon Winery
Source: Photo by Resmo.

a local winery. After a DNA testing of her vines, she learned those vines were very old plants of Mission grapes. There are only ten acres of Mission grapes remaining in California – three of them belong to Deborah.

'I did not know what Mission grapes were,' Deborah told us when we met her in her beautiful ranch in Santa Rita Hills. 'I went to the Archives Library of the Santa Barbara Mission and spent many hours researching the history of the Mission grape.' Her findings brought a new milestone to the history of the Californian wine industry and allowed her to tell a wonderful story on her website (gypsycanyonwinery.com):

> Planted in the late 1800s, it lay hidden and untouched for nearly 100 years. The Mission grape is the Heritage grape of California planted by the Franciscans as they established the California Missions in the 1700s. Today it is the oldest vineyard in Santa Barbara County and cuttings have been donated to Missions throughout California to restore their original Mission vineyards.

Not only did Deborah save the original Mission grapes, but she also discovered a long forgotten wine called Angelica, a fortified dessert wine drunk by the original Californians:

> Angelica is a wine made first in the San Gabriel Mission. On June 17, 1833, Father Duran wrote a letter to Governor Figueroa in which he refers to the wines of the San Gabriel Mission: 'The best wines which I have found in the various missions are those of San Gabriel ... There are also two kinds of white wine. One of them is from pure grapes without fermenting. I mean from pure grape juice without fermenting it with the skins of the pressed grapes. This produces the white wine. The other of the same juice is fermented with a quantity of brandy. These two make the most delicious drink for the dessert. The wine from the pure grape juice is for the altar, the other for any use whatever.'

With further research Deborah found the recipe for the Angelica wine she now produces in her Gypsy Canyon Winery – allowing us to have a taste of what the first Californians were drinking: a sweet fortified wine, supposed to help workers and monks to go through a long, hard day of work, while the regular white wine was served at Mass.

The bottle designed by Deborah is as close as possible in resemblance to the one the first Californians saw (see Figure 1.3): the labels are written by hand and the seal is made of wax. Each bottle is hand-blown, filled and sealed by hand on Deborah's ranch.

Figure 1.3   The bottle designed for Angelica wine
Source: Photo by Resmo.

The 'reasonable' consumption of wine echoed the saying of the Puritan minister Increase Mather: 'Drink is in itself a good Creature of God, and to be received with thankfulness, but the abuse of drink is from Satan; the wine is from God, but the Drunkard is from the Devil.'[7]

Benjamin Franklin, President Thomas Jefferson, spirits and French wines

While California was getting acquainted with wine and food, the East Coast – closer to Europe and the center of political life of a very young country – was more aware of wine culture. 'The rich in New England and Virginia,' writes Barbara Holland, "drank imported wines at considerable expense. One historian reports that 'of these, fiery Madeiras were the favorite of all fashionable folk, and often each glass of wine was strengthened by a liberal dash of brandy.'"[8] Barbara Holland even cites Benjamin Franklin among the best amateurs of Madeira and other alcoholic beverages: 'Imported Madeira had been the beverage of choice for nicer folks; in 1745 Benjamin Franklin penned a jolly drinking ditty concluding, "That virtue and safety in wine-bibbing's found/While all that drink water deserve to be drowned." He said, "Wine makes daily living easier, less hurried, with fewer tensions and more tolerance."'[9] Benjamin Franklin boasted a wine cellar containing more than a thousand bottles, including 258 bottles of red and white Bordeaux and 113 of red Burgundies. A famous story went around the country on the quantity of food and drink the Constitutional Convention was able to consume. In 1776, while the 55 delegates were working hard on the Declaration of Independence, they had dinner in a tavern to gain some rest and relaxation. According to the bill they were sent, they drank 54 bottles of Madeira, 60 bottles of claret, 8 of whiskey, 22 of port, 8 of hard cider and 7 bowls of punch. Restored and merry they went back to work![10]

Like his fellow countryman Benjamin Franklin, President Thomas Jefferson was a wine lover and connoisseur. As early as 1769 he had a small cellar, stocked with the most common wines in colonial America, the hearty Portuguese wines and Madeira. But he strongly believed he could build a home wine industry in America. His dream almost materialized when the Italian wine merchant Philip Mazzei moved to Virginia on Benjamin Franklin's advice. Jefferson gave him 2000 acres to plant European vine cuttings. Optimistic, Mazzei formed the Virginia Wine Company, but the enterprise failed.

Jefferson's interest in wine deepened when he went to France to represent the United States at the Court of Louis XVI in 1784. He took the opportunity to travel in Europe, mostly in Italy and France. He visited Meursault and Montrachet in Burgundy, Condrieu in the Rhone Valley, Turin in Italy, and Bordeaux, where he took a great liking to Margaux, Latour, Haut-Brion and Lafite wines. Seduced by the quality of the wines on offer, he started collecting costly wines from all over France. 'While in Bordeaux, he wrote to inform his brother-in-law Francis Eppes that he had ordered six dozen bottles of Haut-Brion for him, 'of the vintage of 1784, the only very fine one since the year 1779.'[11]

Back in the United States, Jefferson became the herald of French wines and French manners at Monticello. His behavior puzzled his friends and guests, who sometimes bitterly complained about the wine. After politely drinking the claret served by Jefferson at Monticello, one of his guests asked discreetly for a glass of brandy, commenting that 'I have been sipping his d ... d acid, cold French wine, until I am sure I should die in the night unless I take an antidote.'[12]

Indeed, at that time America was drinking hard liquors, sweet wines and beer. When he took the presidency, Jefferson was aware of the tastes of his contemporaries and stocked in his cellar his own favorite wines along with the fortified or sweetened wines like sherry and Madeira dear to his countrymen's palates.

Where did those tastes come from? Madeira and sherry, both sweet tasting, came from Portugal and as such escaped the British blockade during the War of Independence. The American palate became accustomed to the sweetness of the wines. On the other hand, beer and whiskey could both be made from locally grown products, corn or barley, and did not require shipment or a port. In 1795, Jim Beam sold its first barrel of bourbon – founding the first whiskey distillery. Most people drank beer whenever they could get it. That is why wine stayed for many years the privilege of the rich Easterners and a symbol of social status.

Jefferson died without seeing his dream of a mature wine industry come to fruition. But he would be very happy to see that today every one of the 50 States of the Union is making wine, that American wines triumphed over French wines in 1976 – 200 years after Independence – that Château Haut-Brion, his beloved wine, is the property of an American family, having been bought by Clarence Dillon in 1935, and that the latter's son, Douglas, was also the United States of America's Ambassador to France. The links born over 250 years between France and America through wine and culture are still very strong.

Local vineyards and pioneers

Thanks to their European roots and ancestors coming from wine making countries, Americans did not forget their dream of building vineyards. In North Carolina, between 1820 and 1830, John Adlum created the first American 'wine,' which he named 'catawba' in homage to the Native Americans. A London newspaper said in 1857 that it was the best American wine ever created. In California two Frenchmen, Louis Bauchet and Jean-Louis Vignes, introduced some vines from Bordeaux and grafted them onto local vines; immigrants from France, Germany and Italy built the first vineyards in Napa and Sonoma. The first quality vineyards were founded in Napa by three Germans, Charles Krug in 1860, Jacob Schram in 1862 and Gustave Niebaum in 1879; followed by two Italians, Louis Michael Martini in 1933 and Cesare Mondavi in 1943; as well as one Frenchman, Georges de Latour, who founded Beaulieu Vineyard in 1899.

These pioneers of the viticultural industry in the United States came from European countries valuing social wine consumption with the evening meal. True to the culture of their countries of origin, these immigrants were not getting drunk in the local saloon, but had a glass of wine with their evening meal.

These immigrants in turn were counterbalanced by immigrants from Northern Europe, whose Puritan beliefs either discouraged or altogether banned alcohol consumption of any kind. During the colonial years, wine was seen as the major source of inebriation in a rather inaccurate way. Indeed, the truth of the matter was that beer and whiskey were the major sources of alcoholism, but prohibitionist forces linked wine to the ills of American society.

During the nineteenth century, Americans continued to drink a lot of whiskey and beer. Alcoholism was very widespread, and affecting the family life of many households. Men were getting drunk at the saloon where they spent the family money. Rampant drunkenness also increased philandering and violence. A very popular novel, *Ten Nights in a Bar-Room*, published in 1854, became a play and even an early movie. A father spends all his time in a bar, spending the family money and getting drunk, until his young daughter comes to get him. The bartender bashes her on the head and the little girl dies. After this tragedy the father reforms.[13]

This novel reflects the position of the 'Drys,' the non-drinkers opposed to the 'Wets,' the drinkers. Between 1851 and 1860, Maine, Oregon, Massachusetts, Minnesota, Rhode Island, Vermont, Michigan, Connecticut, Delaware, Indiana, Iowa, Nebraska, New Hampshire, New York and Pennsylvania banned all alcoholic beverages. In the 1870s and 1880s women claiming that drunk husbands were hitting their wives and children marched into taverns and saloons to chant hymns and chase men away. The movement expanded until the beginning of the twentieth century.

At the same time the wine industry was booming. Starting in the mid-1850s European vineyards were devastated first by oïdium, then by phylloxera, and American wines were filling the void. By the end of the century the European vineyards had rebounded, but now the American ones were attacked by phylloxera. At the same time prohibitionist attitudes were gaining more and more momentum. In 1917, under the influence of the prohibitionist movement and because of the war, Congress passed the 18th Amendment, banning the commercial production and sale of alcohol in America. In 1920, the Volstead Act was ratified but provided various loopholes. Physicians could prescribe alcohol for medical purposes. A household was legally allowed to produce 200 gallons of wine a year for personal use – a concession to the Italian-American voters – and the Church was allowed to produce wine for religious services.

Because of all these 'concessions' and 'exceptions,' a lot of grape-growers and winemakers were able to survive and even get rich during the Prohibition years. People ordered a lot of grapes to make their own wines while the Church continued ordering wines. Overall, the consumption of wine increased during Prohibition, with whiskey and beer less easily accessible, except in some speakeasies in big cities controlled by the Mafia.

In 1933, Prohibition was repealed, and Congress passed the 21st Amendment. The problem was that Prohibition did not kill America's taste for alcohol, but it had destroyed the distribution system. Indeed, the 21st Amendment transferred the authority to ban or authorize alcohol sales to individual states, with some states choosing to delegate this authority to the county level. Since then the distribution system in the United States has been a nightmare that various legislators and professional lobbies have tried to reform. The legacy of the Prohibition era is a tangle of state and county laws regulating the production and distribution of wine and alcohol, which makes marketing a difficult and frustrating task even today.

After the Repeal, wine consumption dropped and Americans went back to drinking whiskey and beer. To these two traditional drinks they now added dessert and fortified wines with a high percentage of alcohol. These fortified wines were very cheap and catered to the 'misery market.' Parallel to this market, immigrant families from the Old World wine-producing countries continued to drink wines during their meals, but their children began drinking beer and whiskey as they integrated into the American way of life. To most Americans wine was still a mysterious beverage, associated with high-society status.

In the early 1960s, the American sweet tooth switched from strong semi-sweet fortified wines to dessert or sweet wines like white Zinfandel. This transitional generation included the young 'baby boomers' coming of age, more traveled, more educated and sophisticated than their elders. Even so, they bought simple, often sweet, wines.

As they grew older they benefitted from the development of the wine industry. In the 1980s the American wine industry was internationally recognized. The famous 'Judgment of Paris' had shown the world that California could create very high quality wine in a very competitive environment. Wine was not the mysterious beverage reserved for the rich and famous, but was a drink everyone could share or experiment with among friends and family. At the same time American chefs were becoming famous for their cooking, and in a natural progression, wine and food pairing became a fashionable exercise.

At the end of the twentieth century, 75 million Baby Boomers were getting interested in wine. They were drinking less beer and more wine. But the culture of wine and food is still very different from one area to another, as is shown in Figure 1.4, a map of culinary America.

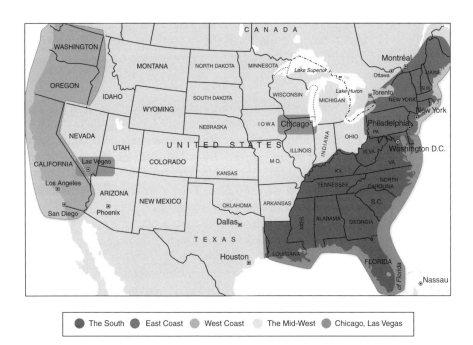

Figure 1.4 Map of culinary America
Source: Resmo.

American tastes changed over the centuries because of immigration and the influences of other countries. In Figure 1.4, four major culinary areas are defined:

- The South, influenced by Caribbean and African cultures. It gave birth to Cajun cuisine as well as all those fabulous African foods, like gumbos etc.
- The more traditionalist East Coast, with descendants from the Pilgrims and heir to British culture.
- The contemporary West Coast, open to many influences, Mexico, Japan, China and India;
- The Mid-Western world is more strictly traditionalist and usually pro-hibitionist. It is the world that certainly inherited most of the colonial food traditions. Since the publication of James McWilliams's book, *A Revolution In Eating: How the Quest for Food Shaped America* (April, 2005), we know much more accurately how America fed itself during the colonial years. Dr. James McWilliams, professor at the University of San Marcos, Texas, studied the impact of Native American traditions on the cooking of the pioneers, and how the geography of the Great Plains impacted on the way the pioneers had to adapt to their new surroundings. That is how rice, corn, sugar cane and wheat became part of the American diet. The Native Americans influenced the way the first Americans cooked and built their kitchens:

> On a warm spring afternoon in 1650, Rebecca Cole stepped out of her garden, entered her kitchen, and began to cook. Maryland, where the Cole family had migrated from Middlesex, England, was becoming well known not only for its profitable tobacco crops but also for its ample corn, abundant garden vegetables, and healthy supply of meat. And that combination, as it did on most days, would make up the evening meal. Rebecca had started soaking corn kernels at the crack of dawn to soften them for pounding, an exhausting task made necessary by the lack of a local gristmill. She knew that she needed about six cups of cornmeal to feed her husband, five children and herself. So for the next couple of hours, Rebecca and her two daughters dutifully hunched over a large mortar, took wooden pestles in hand, and reduced a tub of white corn kernels into a gritty heap of meal. Meanwhile, out in the barn, Robert Cole and his son, Robert Jr., contemplated a decision: pork or beef?[14]

Finally, we consider two cosmopolitan cities shown on our map, Las Vegas and Chicago, whose taste for wine and food sets them apart from the other areas.

Case Study: Chicago, 'big shoulders,
open minds, sharp palates'[15]

For many decades Chicago was the city of hot dogs and deep-dish pizza.
It is also famous for having resisted Prohibition – quite illegally, of
course, under the strong and cruel supervision of the infamous Al
Capone. Today, Chicago is spoken about for its great chefs, its talented
sommeliers and its great food inspired by traditions from all over the
American and European continents.

Journalist Paul Hart pays tribute to the French influence in Chicago:

> Louis Joliet and Father Jacques Marquette were the first explorers to visit in
> the late 1600s what would become Chicago. Chicago's first permanent set-
> tler, the Haitian-French Jean-Baptiste Point Du Sable, came here in 1780. The
> French influence still reigns in the form of top restaurants like Everest,
> Michael's (thanks to chef/owner Michael Lachowicz, a sauce genius), and
> Les Nomades, a Chicago dining institution operated by the incomparable
> Mary Beth Liccione … The city's modern fine-dining scene first came to the
> notice of the world with the arrival of another Frenchman, Jean Banchet, in
> 1973, the year he founded Le Français … In its heyday, well-heeled business-
> men would fly in to a small, local airport to sample the best French cuisine in
> the country.[16]

This French tradition is still carried on by Mark Grosz, chef owner of
Oceanique, who learned his trade at Le Francais with Jean Banchet. After
his apprenticeship, Grosz went on to work in France and Hong Kong,
widening the spectrum of his imagination.

In addition to French restaurants, Chicago hosts Alinea, founded by
chef owner Grant Achatz who travels 'through the culinary halls of
America.' The wine director Joe Catterson tries to match his extensive
wine list with the creative 12 to 24 course-tasting menus, which change
every three months.

Leaving America, let us now go to Italy with chef Tony Mantuano, co-
owner of Spiaggia. He looks for inspiration to Italy, where he travels several times a year and chooses wines with his sommelier Steven
Alexander: 'My goal,' says Alexander, 'is for our customers to be drinking wines that they would be drinking in Italy – which is very much in
keeping with the chef's inspiration for the restaurant as a whole.'

America, en route to a new way of drinking?

The food scene in America is changing the way Americans relate to wine
and food. Americans are becoming more discriminating, more open to

new flavors and new aromas, they are slowly but surely moving towards new tastes, new wines, new habits of consumption. More traveled and with more savvy than his ancestors, the twenty-first-century American is a new consumer – fed by the Internet, the *Wine Spectator* and wonderful wineries all over the country.

If not attracted to international wines, Americans now have the choice from American wineries. Since 2005, every US state has had at least one winery (see Table 1.2). Even Alaska has six wineries!

Table 1.2   US wineries, 1975–2007

Year	Total US wineries	Nr states with wineries
1975	579	34
1995	1,817	47
2005	3,820	50
2006	4,280	50
2007	4,712	50

Over a period of 20 years between 1975 and 1995, the number of wineries tripled. Over a period of ten years from 1995 to 2005, the number doubled. In the two years from 2005 to 2007, it increased by around 30 percent.[17]

Japan: a taste for Old Europe

This is the country where the two terms 'art' and 'living' come together and are full of meaning. The act of eating is very ritualized, with the ritual being very old and undergoing little change over time. This tradition holds the key to why wine has become increasingly important in recent times.

Between the sixth and eighth centuries, Japan had very strong ties with China and was very much influenced by Chinese culture. Chinese cuisine was based on Buddhist principles, a religion based on respect for all forms of life. This explains why, for many centuries, the Japanese diet was completely vegetarian. Chinese influence ended in the middle of the ninth century when the Tang dynasty disappeared.

The next century saw the birth of the golden age of Japan, called Heian from the name Heian-Kyo, the ancient Japanese capital city, now Kyoto. For 400 years, the art of living was at its height and the etiquette code was created. The food diet was still frugal, but the elegance of the table setting, the tableware and the cutlery made up for any deficiencies in the food by the visual elegance. Later on, the samurai era introduced even more elegance and eating became a real art and even a ceremony.

In the fifteenth century Japan came in contact with the Western world, and more specifically with Portugal, a nation of explorers and discoverers. Japanese people learned how to fry food from the Portuguese invaders. Shocked by the heavy taste of the fried Portuguese food, they refined it to a light and elegant tempura. But Japan resisted introducing meat into their diet until the end of the nineteenth century.

The basic principles of a meal are:

- presenting the food raw, which requires the ingredients to be extremely fresh;
- elegant visual presentation of the food in containers of glass, wood, lacquer or bamboo, and matching or contrasting colors.

There are now three types of meals:

- the *Kaiseki*, ritual meal inspired by the Zen tradition and the samurai
- the traditional meal
- the *bento*

The *Kaiseki* meal is regarded as the most exquisite culinary refinement in Japan. The dishes are mainly composed of vegetables and fish with seaweed and mushrooms as the seasoning base, and are characterized by their refined flavor.

The typical Japanese meal consists of a bowl of rice, one of miso soup, pickled vegetables and fish or meat. While rice is the staple food, several kinds of noodles (udon, soba and ramen) are cheap and very popular for light meals. Japan being an island, a wide variety of fish, squid, octopus, eel and shellfish are readily available for every meal.

The *bento* is a meal ready to go, packed as a picnic. The tradition dates back to the sixth century, when the shogun gave rice and marinated vegetable rations to his troops before going to war.

The drinking habits are very coded and specific to a culture that does not drink wine but a lot of strong spirits, beer and tea. In cozy and friendly Japanese-style bars, customers often pour drinks for each other from bottles of beer as a gesture of companionship. If you are a fellow beer drinker, reciprocate with your own bottle. A whiskey drinker may invite you to drink from his bottle and fix a drink for you. In this case, you need not reciprocate unless you have your own bottle. Many of these bars have a bottle-keep system for regular patrons, who buy a bottle from time to time, as it is less expensive than paying for single drinks in the long run.

Japanese sake (rice wine) goes extremely well with a variety of Japanese dishes. Brewed with rice and water, sake has been a Japanese alcoholic beverage since ancient times. It can be drunk warm or cold. When drunk chilled, good sake has a taste similar to fine-quality wine. There are local sake breweries in every region across the country, which make their respective characteristic tastes based on the quality of rice and water as well as differences in the brewing process.

Wine is definitely an acquired taste for Japanese. Table 1.3 shows what Japanese consumers drank in 2003 while Table 1.4 shows how their consumption evolved from 1992 to 2002.

Japan has a tradition of breweries. The three most important are the Asahi Breweries, the Kirin Breweries, the Sapporo Breweries, and there is one wine and spirits company, Suntory. Japanese law authorizes wines

Table 1.3 Japanese consumption of alcohol in 2003 (percent)

Type	Percentage share
Sake + synthetic sake	9.6
Shochu (base for cocktails)	9.9
Mirin	1.1
Beer	41.5
Fruit wines	2.7
Whiskey	1.0
Brandy	0.1
Happoshu (sort of beer, less alcohol)	27.2
Liquors	6.3
Spirits	0.5

Table 1.4 The evolution of Japanese consumption, 1992–2002

Category	1992	1997	2000	2001	2002
Sake	14.8	11.5	9.8	9.3	8.8
Synthetic sake	0.3	0.5	0.6	0.6	0.6
Schochu	5.9	7.1	7.4	7.9	8.3
Mirin	0.9	1.0	1.4	1.0	1.0
Beer	74.1	64.8	52	46.1	41.1
Wine	1.3	2.4	2.8	2.7	2.7
Whiskey and brandy	2.5	1.7	1.5	1.3	1.2
White Spirits	0.4	0.3	0.3	0.3	0.3
Liqueurs	1.4	2.5	3.8	4.5	5.4
Happoshu	0.1	4.5	16.0	21.7	24.7

made from various fruit, including grapes. Imports are very important in the wine and spirits industry: imported wines are up to 62.4 percent, and come mostly from France, followed by Italy and Spain.

Who has the most influence on Japanese wine drinkers?

In the wine industry, as well as among customers, it is very often said that critics and journalists have too much influence on consumers and trade. In Japan the most influential critic is Joe Satake, a fictional character. Created by Araki Joh, Shinobu Kaitani and Ken-Ichi Hori in a manga (a sort of comics for adults), Joe Satake is a sommelier, son of a Japanese father and a French mother. A lot of his adventures take place in France or are about French wines, the favorite wines of Japanese consumers. Joe has such a fine nose he can identify a so-called Bordeaux mixed with Rioja wine, discern a difference between a 1983 and a 1985 Champagne or recognize between two so-called vintages of the famed Domaine de la Romanée Conti … one of which is really a Pinot Noir from California. A mean competitor had tried to trick him by substituting one of the two Romanée Conti with the Jensen Cuvée of Calera vineyards. The story does not end there. Joe is so successful and such an authority for his readers that the Calera Pinot Noir became the rage among young wine drinkers. When winemaker Jensen came to Tokyo, he spent hours signing empty bottles while his importer was thrilled by the resulting sudden rise of Calera Pinot Noir sales!

New markets

The United States and Japan are mature markets for wine because there is already a wine drinking tradition in those countries. It is not quite the case with new and emerging wine-drinking countries such as China, India and Russia, just to name the three that make the headlines in the wine press.

China: opening to wine

China is such a huge country that there are as many cuisines as there are regions. A Chinese proverb sums up the problem in a few words: 'In the East, sweet and mild; in the West, spicy and hot; in the North, salty and copious; in the South, fresh and delicate.'

Food in China and rice wine

In the Guizhou province, the food is fiery and hot. It is usually eaten with a very strong spirit, called Maotai. Maotai is about 53° strong and the province produces about 1300 liters a year. The Maotai is a grain spirit distilled from wheat and sorghum. The brandy ages for many years in cellars and is sold in delicate ceramic bottles with a white, red and golden label. It is drunk in all the great occasions, a public banquet, a business meal or a public festivity. Even now that the imports of cognac and whiskey are increasing, the Maotai is preferred by the Chinese.

In the Yunnan province (see Figure 1.5), the vegetables are varied and fresh, and they are served with a bitter-sweet sauce or accompaniment. The province has one delicate dish, the 'Yunnan Mixlan,' fine rice noodles in a very spicy sauce.

Figure 1.5　Map of China

In Hunan, the cuisine is also known as 'Xiang,' named after the fabulous river crossing the province and it is very hot and spicy. During a meal peppers are served as an accompaniment. Hunan cuisine is based on meat, such as duck, mutton and goose. Very little fish is served, except some from the river.

Sichuan is known for its pepper, and because the food is spicy it is very often served with beer or rice wine. Rice wine is deeply ingrained in the Chinese culture. It is not considered a wine but simply as a drink. That is why Chinese people toast with rice wine and then drain their glass. That is called 'gam bei,' which means 'dry glass,' and it is considered rude not to participate.

A long history of wine

Contrary to Japan that has no wine tradition, wine goes far back in Chinese history. But Communism destroyed all memory of this ancient history. Pieter Eijkhoff writes:

> Many Westerners are familiar with Japanese sake but few will know that it represents a type of alcoholic drink, which has only ever been made in China and Japan (where it was introduced from China). Sake is neither a wine nor a spirit. Some sake made today has been strengthened with spirit, but sake itself is a type of alcohol known in China as chiu, of which a very rough translation is 'strong beer.' Ordinary beer, with an alcohol content reaching perhaps 4 or 5 per cent, has been made throughout the world for thousands of years. It was known to the Egyptians and Babylonians, and mention of it as an offering to the spirits in sacrifices occurs in early bone inscriptions in China dated about 1500 BC. There were many different kinds of this ordinary beer, with varying ingredients, from assorted regions.[18]

> Readers will be doubly surprised to learn that the Chinese invented brandy, because though the fact in itself is impressive enough, it is not widely realized that the Chinese drank wine made from grapes at all, much less distilled it into brandy. Grape wine was being drunk by the second century BC at the latest in China, since we begin to have textual evidence of it by then. The envoy and traveler Chang Ch'ien brought good wine grapes (*Vitis vinifera*) back with him from Bactria about 126 BC. Before the importation of those grapes, however, there were wild vine species, or 'mountain grapes,' which were already being used for wine, namely *Vitis thunbergii* and *Vitas filifolia*. Wine made from them is mentioned before Chang Ch'ien in the book called *Classical Pharmacopoeia of the Heavenly Husbandman*.[19]

The assertions of Dr. Eijkhof are contradicted by some linguists. There is no real word in Chinese for 'wine.' Traditionally, the Chinese word for 'wine' can mean any kind of alcoholic beverage ranging from rice wines to grape wines and sometimes even beer. Therefore when speaking about wine one has to specify 'grape wine.' Furthermore, the variety names of many occidental grapes have not been translated in Chinese. Worse, many native grape varieties have not yet been translated into any occidental language. Confusion will continue to be the norm as long as we do not have a Chinese wine dictionary.

In spite of all those difficulties, there are more than 500 wineries in China, representing 83 percent of the total consumption while the other 17 percent are imports. Table 1.5, below, shows these wineries.

Table 1.5 also shows that wine and alcohol have been part of Chinese traditions for a long time. The largest wineries are spending millions to advertise on TV and to sell their wines. But, like the Japanese, the Chinese do not drink with their meals. They drink before or after or in-between, but not with. However, their consumption is increasing,

Table 1.5   Chinese wineries

Name	Brand	Location	Date of creation
Yantai Winery	Yantai	Yantai, Shandong Province	1985
Sino-Japanese Friendship Winery		Yantai	1985
Beijing Winery	Zhongghuo	Beijing	1910
Dragon Seal Wines Corp.	Dragon Seal	Beijing	1987
Qingdao Huaguan	Qingdao	Qingdao	1914
Huadong Winery	Huadong	Laoshan, Qingdao	1985
Great Wall Wine Co.	Great Wall	Shacheng, Hebei Province	1960
Dynasty Winery	Dynasty	Tianjin, Golf Bo Hai	1980
Tonghua Winery	Tonghua	Jilin Province	–
Zhe Jiang Cereals, Oils and Foodstuff	Pagoda	Hangzhou	–
Dong Ni	Quingdao Dongni Winery	Quingdao	–
Chuanyan	Chuan Wine	Sichuan	–
Hong	Yuquan Winery	Nixia	–
Mogao	LingZhou Winery	Ganzu	–
Lou Lan	Shanshan Winery	Xinjiang	–

following the rise of a more important middle class earning between US\$5,000 and US\$13,000 annually. This middle class was virtually non-existent ten years ago, and now represents 9 percent of the population, that is, 30,000,000 people. With the 2008 Olympics, dozens of luxury hotels and restaurants are being built around Beijing. The Chinese government is also encouraging the move from hard liquor to wine, and keeps lowering import taxes to encourage this.

Luckily for France, the Chinese still think that French wines are the best. That is why importers of the Classified Growths and all the luxury wines are selling their wines with no problem – sometimes even more expensively than in Europe or in the United States! Wine is definitively on its way in China.

Luxury wines: a new market in China?

On April 18, 2007, some very happy Chinese people in Beijing tasted Chateau Haut-Brion blanc and Chateau Haut-Brion rouge: 'it tastes better than rice wine or beer, and it's better for your health,' said one of the lucky participants. Those words are milk and honey to the ears of many importers and owners of wine estates. Prince Robert of Luxembourg, whose family owns Chateau Haut-Brion, is aware of the growing interest of Chinese executives for luxury wines: 'I think people are starting to understand the notion of quality brands. The luxury brand has ignited interest in the Chinese market. There's been a lot of work done by a lot of these luxury groups – they're very visible here. I think the timing is right for us.'

Of course the market is still very small, but it is expanding dramatically. In 2005, China jumped into the world's top ten wine-consuming countries. In 2006 Chinese wine imports doubled over the previous year, from 1.15 million cases to 2.2 million, and, with annual consumption at a mere 0.7 liters per person, there is plenty of room for growth. No wonder wine-market analysts foresee a 36 percent increase in Chinese wine imports by 2010.

The road to India

India is another emerging, and very promising, market for the wine industry. Like China, India does not have a real wine culture, but is developing a taste for occidental wines.

India's drink and food traditions are very much influenced by the various cultures that crossed its history, but there are unifying trends, like the use of spices and many similar ingredients. Generally speaking, Indian cuisine can be divided into four main areas: North Indian, South Indian, East Indian and West Indian (see Figure 1.6).

North Indian cuisine is distinguished by a heavier use of dairy products; milk, clarified butter and yogurt. The staple food in most of North India is a variety of lentils, vegetables, and wheat-based bread, called *roti*. Some common North Indian foods such as the various kebabs and most of the meat dishes originated with Muslim arrival in the country. Since Pakistan was part of North India prior to the partition of the country, Pakistani cuisine is very similar to Northern Indian cuisine.

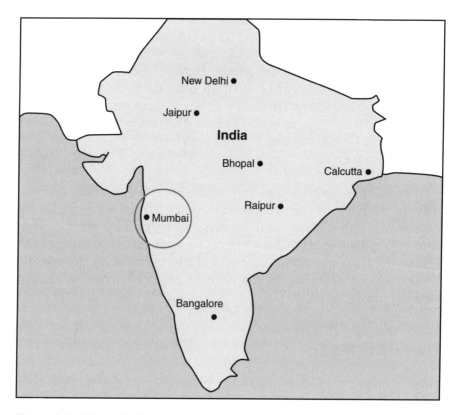

Figure 1.6 Map of India

East Indian cuisines employ thickening agents such as cashew or poppy seed paste. Fish and seafood are very popular in the coastal states of Orissa and West Bengal. Many of the sweet dishes now popular in Northern India initially originated in the Bengal region.

South Indian cuisine is distinguished by a greater emphasis on rice, the use of coconut, and particularly coconut oil, and curry leaves.

Tea is the main beverage throughout India; the finest varieties being grown in Darjeeling and Assam, and is generally prepared as *masala chai*, that is, a tea with a mixture of spices boiled in milk. The second most popular beverage, coffee, is largely served in South India. Other beverages include lemonade (*nimbu pani*), *lassi*, or milk with nuts and cardamom. India also has many local alcoholic beverages, including palm wine and Indian beer. However, the practice of drinking a beverage with a meal is not traditional in India.

The next emerging market after China

Since the British days of the Raj, an Indian couple's social prestige and reputation as good hosts were determined by the Scotch they served to their guests. For decades, Scotch was the tipple of choice, prized, relished and coveted above all other drinks. Wine was a horrendously alien brew, found only in the homes of rich *cognoscente*, who dabbled in such exotica.

Those days are now over, but Indians still drink only five million bottles a year – a mere half a teaspoon per capita – as against the lakes of whisky, rum and vodka that are consumed. There are an estimated 200 million regular whisky drinkers, compared with 700,000 regular wine drinkers, but a shift is under way.

Indians consumed more than 220 million cases of beer and other spirits in 2006. The market grew by 10 percent. Indian-made foreign liquor (whiskey, gin, rum and vodka) accounted for half the market. Beer dominated, with 90 percent of the rest of the market.

Wines grew by nearly 25 percent, but in comparison to whiskey, where 60 million cases were sold, wines sales were only 650,000 cases. The whiskey market, like that of wine, is one of the fastest growing in the world.

Russia: from vodka to wine

In spite of a reputation for hard drinking, Russians are way behind the French, Irish and Czechs in alcohol consumption, with only 9.3 liters a year per capita. Russian traditions in wine and food explain this bad reputation, and the current situation. As the author of the online Wikipedia article on 'Russian cuisine' explains:

> Russian cuisine derives its rich and varied character from the vast and multicultural expanse of Russia. Its foundations were laid by the peasant food of the rural population in an often harsh climate, with a combination of plentiful fish, poultry, game, mushrooms, berries, and honey. Crops of rye, wheat, barley, and millet provided the ingredients for a plethora of breads, pancakes, cereals, kvass, beer, and vodka. Flavorful soups and stews centered on seasonal or storable produce, fish, and meats. This wholly native food remained the staples for the vast majority of Russians well into the 20th century. Lying on the northern reaches of the ancient Silk Road, as well as Russia's close proximity to the Caucasus, Persia, and the Ottoman Empire has provided an inescapable Eastern character to its cooking methods (not so much in European Russia but distinguishable in the North Caucasus).

Later on, from the sixteenth to the eighteenth century, Russians imported smoked meats and fish, pastry cooking, salads and green vegetables, chocolate, ice cream, wines and liquor. This created, for the rich and mighty aristocrats, the various sources of refined and elegant dishes. This trend was confirmed and extended in the nineteenth century, when the Russian court and aristocracy imported not only the ingredients but also the French and Austrian personnel able to cook the new dishes. That is why, concludes our anonymous author of the Wikipedia article, 'Many of the foods that are considered in the West to be traditionally Russian actually come from the Franco-Russian cuisine of the 18th and 19th centuries, and include such widespread dishes as Veal Orloff, Beef Stroganoff, and Sharlotka (Charlotte Russe).'[20]

It was customary for the traditional Russian to drink mostly vodka with his meals. Thirty years ago, Russians were drinking 17 liters of wine per capita a year. The rest of their alcoholic consumption was dedicated to beer and vodka. By the mid-1990s, their wine consumption had plummeted to 2.5 liters, but went back up to 5.1 liters in 1998. The main core of their consumption is still vodka and beer.

Conclusion

The traditions of wine and food in traditional as well as emerging markets press a heavy weight on the wine industry. But the world is changing, as well as traditions evolving under the influence of younger generations and the new technologies. Is it possible for a marketer or a communications expert to imagine the future of this industry? Maybe not, but some people did some preliminary work, such as Patrick Dixon in his *Futurewise* book.

CHAPTER 2

Values and trends of the new consumers

The traditional wine consumer is dead! Long live the New Consumer! Changing patterns in the everyday life of consumers affect their values and trends. These global changes apply to the local consumer in his local environment, and create new trends and values common to consumers all over the world. In today's world, they are global consumers.

Dr. Patrick Dixon is one of the major business thinkers in Europe. He is often described in the media as Europe's leading Futurist, and has been ranked as one of the 20 most influential business thinkers alive today. Originally a physician by training, Dr. Dixon has a Web TV site and a radio/TV studio in his home from which he broadcasts worldwide for the BBC and others. His major work, *Futurewise*, first published in 1998, reached its fourth edition in 2007.

In this book, Dr. Dixon describes how the future stands in his mind, in terms of what he calls the 'six faces of the future':

F ast
U rban
T ribal
U niversal
R adical
E thic

This structure can easily be applied to the new wine consumer in the Western world as well as in various emerging markets.

Patrick Dixon's book, *Futurewise*

Dr. Dixon's book focusses on our future world, and is constantly being revised by its author. Dr. Dixon studies all the topics and aspects of what our world will look like in the next 10, 15, 25 or 50 years, and the influence that money, war, terrorism, media, consumerism, water supplies, pollution and so on will have on emerging trends.

These are not, of course, subjects for a book on web marketing and wine branding. But Dr. Dixon's book provides a very interesting pattern perfectly applicable to the wine business and its consumers. Indeed, the transformations of society impact considerably on the behavioral patterns of wine consumers as well as on the industry's marketing. The changes in society force both marketers and academics to rethink their strategy, and to include the Web as one of the major marketing tools.

In his introduction to *Futurewise*, Patrick Dixon makes a very deep distinction between pre-millennialists and post-millennialists, calling the latter the 'M Generation': 'Pre-millennialists tend to see 2000 to 2020 as just another couple of decades. The trends of the 1980s and 1990s continue, just more of the same. Post-millennialists are very different. They are products of the third millennium. They live in it. They are twenty-first-century people, a new age.'[1] Why? Because they will spend all their adult life in the new millennium. It is these 'Millennials' who fascinate the wine industry and every brand.

This difference between pre- and post-millennialists also explains why there are trends and counter-trends. There are universal and tribal trends, urban and radical (as in 'roots') trends, fast and ethical trends. 'The big question is: If trend and counter-trend coexist, which will be dominant in the new millennium? 'The truth is,' answers Patrick Dixon, 'that in a pluralistic, multitrack society there are a number of pendulums operating and each creates new business opportunities.'[2]

That is why Dixon breaks society down into two distinct groups, one group composed of the Universal Fast Urban type, the other consisting of the Tribal Ethical Radical type.

Universal	**Tribal**
Fast	**Ethical**
Urban	**Radical**

These two human groups are not competitive because they ignore each other. The urban executive, traveling half of the time from country to country and living out of a suitcase in major cities, has no, or very little, contact with an individual living within his/her group or tribe, having ethical concerns and being rooted in his/her way. This small minority should not be ignored, because it is very often, as Dr. Dixon points out, the driving force towards major changes. As we go along in this chapter, we will sum up briefly what Dr. Dixon meant – as we have understood it – and figure out what points are really relevant to our topic.

This chapter is not about building a new world, or trying to figure out what the wine business will look like in the next ten years. We are using Dr. Dixon's pattern to give as accurate an image as possible of wine consumers today in most of the countries where wine is consumed.

F – as in fast

The international consumer lives in a fast world: fast-changing technologies, fast-changing products, fast-changing world, fast food, fast travels. Dixon sums up in a striking sentence, 'The developed world, is cash-rich, time-poor and intensely impatient.'[3]

The rise of the Internet is certainly one of the most significant changes in the way consumers can access new products, new information and new people. News now travels almost instantaneously, as the phenomenon of 'breaking news' on the American news channel CNN shows. Consumers are used to zapping from one TV channel to another, and apply the zapping technique to brands. They are not loyal to a brand anymore and keep changing, depending on the ad, the novelty or the appeal.

Because the technology is changing, so too, is the market changing. The consumer requests diversity and quality, as well as immediate access to the product he wants to buy, taste or try. The answer is e-commerce or the sale of goods online.

Yesterday, Europeans were drinking their fathers' cellars and building cellars for their children. The Americans were recovering from the Repeal of Prohibition and were building their wine industry. The Japanese were recovering from World War II and getting acquainted with Europe. Today, the French, Americans and the Japanese are 'zapping' from one wine to another, experimenting with new tastes, new countries and new styles.

Yesterday, the French were drinking 80 liters a year; today they are drinking 55 liters a year. Americans were almost exclusively drinking beer, cocktails and whiskey; they are now drinking 8 liters of wine a year. The Japanese were drinking sake and tea; now they are drinking French classified growths and other European fine wines.

Yesterday, wine was served everyday at lunch and dinner in Europe. Today, the French, the Americans and the Japanese are eating sandwiches in front of their computers, reaching for the bottle of water and the cup of coffee. Dinner time is very often some frozen food reheated in the microwave by an overworked parent, or some pizza ordered by phone and delivered to the door.

Yesterday, before the family meal, Mr. Dupont went into his cellar, chose his bottle carefully and put it on the table to complement the nice dinner home-cooked by Mrs. Dupont. Today, Mrs. Dupont chooses the wine and gets in her car to buy it at the nearest supermarket. Yesterday, Mr. Smith was drinking beer and Mrs. Smith milk. Today, they are all drinking sodas, beers or wine.

Yesterday, regional branding was an important element to help wine enthusiasts develop an understanding of the global wine world. Today, the New World favors varietal wines, while the Old World is switching strategy.

Today, all of them – Japanese, Europeans, Americans, Indians, Chinese, Russians – are connected by telephone and through the Internet, and to the Internet through their cellphones. The M Generation of Patrick Dixon could also be called the 'Mobile Generation,' because their mobile phones connect them to the world through the Internet. The M Generation can buy online by phone after they have found the information they were looking for on the Internet.

Because it is connected to the world by phone 24 hours a day, seven days a week if it wants to be, the M generation is also a giant online community. Ben and Linda Smith, two young Americans interested in wine, are connected to the Internet. Their counterparts in Europe are Pierre and Sylvie Dupont, in India Chandra Singh and in China Yin Li. All those people are going to surf the Net to find information on wine, exchange ideas and tips or share their tasting notes on their favorite wines or addresses of good wine and e-commerce sites.

What do those people living in different cultures and speaking different languages have in common? Mostly, they share the same interest in wine, food and a quality lifestyle, speak English or have a reasonable grasp of English and have access to the Internet. Sooner or later they will cross paths on a forum, on a blog or on an informational site on wine. They will be part of community-building projects, such as wine encyclopedias, wikis, blogs or forums. 'The spirit of the online community,' explains Patrick Dixon, 'will continue to be a passionate belief that information should whenever possible be given away for the benefit of humankind as a whole. This ethic will have a profound effect on many businesses ....'[4]

Dr. Dixon can now switch to the present tense. Almost everyday a new site is born to sustain the international online community of wine consumers. Wine forums, wine blogs and even wikis are now so popular that their numbers have exploded. The latest community we heard of is a wiki allowing tasting notes to be shared. What is a wiki? A wiki is a text written by several authors; everybody can contribute to the work, provided they share the sources of their information and have a decent knowledge of the subject. The most famous example of such a work is the *Wikipedia*, which is an encyclopedia first written in English, but now available in several languages by people who are passionate or knowledgeable about a subject. Access to the encyclopedia is totally free. Of course, academics and teachers very often question the quality of the information, but the purpose of the Wikipedia is to give as much information as possible, which is as reliable as possible, at no cost to the web surfer.

The wiki on wine tasting, WineApe.com, was founded in 2006 by Jeff Dracup, Colleen Wagner and Kevin Jackson – three people who enjoy trying new wines, but who found that most wines had no rating. Their idea is to challenge the power of the wine critics, and to give the power to the consumers. Why should consumers choose their wines only on the advice of a few wine critics, who have access to a limited number of bottles? There are two important reasons why not. 'First, the ratings come from a select group of people who may or may not have the same taste in wine as the average consumer. Second, and more importantly, there are just too many wines being released each year for all wines to be rated by such a small group of wine tasters. As a consequence, we found that the vast majority of wines have no rating,' said Jeff Dracup, Co-Founder/ CEO of WineApe.[5]

The idea behind WineApe.com is to create an international community of wine tasters/consumers who share their tasting notes with everybody. Not only will this community bypass the wine critics, who publish in print or even on the Net at very carefully chosen times (to be ahead of competition), but the community will help winemakers to know their consumers better. The ratings of their wines by their consumers are included in emails that go to the wineries. 'We're hoping these emails will provide wineries with the feedback from consumers necessary to help wineries improve their wines and offer better wine values,' says Colleen Wagner, President of WineApe.[6]

Fast to inform, fast to react, fast to form his/her own opinion, here is the new consumer of the twenty-first century.

U – as in urban

Who has not heard of the giant metropolises of Europe, China or North and South America? Huge industrialized cities are the current trend; think London, think Los Angeles, think Beijing, think Mumbai and you get the picture. Pollution, millions of people milling around, very poor people living alongside but invisible to rich people, new millionaires and billionaires, people starving and dying of misery and disease, this is the apocalyptic picture of strong contrasts drawn by Dr. Dixon.

For the wealthiest, the trend is to live in the city, where there are business opportunities and leisure. But the counter-trend is for other sections of the wealthiest, tired of the noise and the pollution, to move to the country, to 'go back' to nature (while maintaining a place in the city for the buzz and the energy). The less rich will move to suburbs to have more green, more safety, more spacious homes, and they will commute. But now they can work at home and get organized. The M Generation will make sure they can telework, run their virtual companies and meet through the Internet, instead of flying or driving.

How does this apply to the wine consumer? Staying home to work, not driving or flying, not exercising; these have an impact on the urban citizen's health, food, drink and diet. If recent scenarios are anything to go by, we can expect scares about food poisoning, obesity, the dangers of overdrinking and overeating, as well as neurotic eaters and drinkers wanting to stay 'slim' and starving themselves. There will be people starving in Africa with no water and no regular food supplies, people abandoning their roots or traditions to become addicted to foreign lifestyles, new millionaires trying to imitate the worst behaviors of their Western counterparts.

These trends and counter-trends sustain an urban style of wine drinking and eating. On November 17, 1991, CBS's '60 Minutes' broadcast included a report on the correlation between French consumption of red wine and lower rates of heart disease. The segment popularized and legitimized the 'French Paradox.' Scores of Americans immediately went running to wine stores during the four weeks following the initial broadcast, resulting in a 44 percent increase in sales of red wine in US supermarkets. They just forgot the other side of the coin. The 'French Paradox' was a set of basic rules for a balanced diet, including fiber intake from vegetables and fruits, natural sugars derived from the consumption of carbohydrates such as cereals, rice, potatoes or noodles in moderate quantity, and proteins from eating a lot of fish, but very little meat and fat. The 'French Paradox' does not include snacks, sodas, sugar and chocolate at every meal or on a daily basis.

Over the following years, the 'French Paradox' encouraged some urban and sophisticated Americans to change their diet. The Cretan or Mediterranean diet became trendy. Olive oil, carbohydrates, vegetables, fruit, fish and red wine were the elements contributing to health and a long life.

The only advantage of this 'French Paradox' trend was the renewed interest of Americans in wine and their switch to it from beer and hard liquors. It also changed the way people drank wine. Even if Americans (like their Chinese, Indian and Japanese counterparts) drank mostly away from home in bars or restaurants, they started buying wine for special occasions at home or for a weekly dinner.

T – as in tribal

'Tribalism creates belonging, identity, family, community, teams and nations ...,' wrote Dr. Dixon. 'Tribalism provides a sense of identity. Tribalism helps us understand who we are, where we've come from and where we're headed. Teams are to do with tasks, tribes are about whole groups moving together.'[7] It is possible to go even further: tribalism has two almost contradictory characteristics – it can be 'horizontal' or 'vertical.'

Horizontal tribalism

Because some people have lost their physical roots through mobility, they feel the need to belong to a tribe centered on their hobbies, personal tastes or beliefs. There are now many tribes: young, gay, female, African-American, Hispanic, baby boomers, seniors and so on. This horizontal (or transversal) tribalism respects local or specific cultures.

The Hispanic community in the United States is a growing target. It is the largest minority group with over 39 million people, of whom 65 percent were born in the United States. Hispanics under the age of 35 spend over $300 billion annually. For many marketers this is the most misunderstood minority – maybe because it is the least known and most untapped market. In the United States, Hispanic culture is both rich and very diverse. Marketers cannot target the Mexican, the Cuban or the Puerto Rican communities in the same way just because basically they all speak the same language. To make it even more complex, the American Hispanic community is composed of Hispanic people speaking both English and Spanish, some being totally integrated into the American way of life if they are second- or third-generation immigrants, with many of them spread over several American states: California,

Texas, Florida, New York, to name a few. Mass marketing in Spanish will not provide the right answer.

A Californian winery answered the problem with a very interesting strategy. Considering that Hispanic people were more and more interested in wine, in 2004 Round Hill Winery launched a promotional campaign designed specifically for this demographic. The 'Bolsa de Recetas,' or 'Purse of Recipes,' was created to appeal to the Latino or Latina consumer as a gift. The 'Bolsa,' which is sold on bottles of Round Hill wine, featured a variety of recipes in a colorful and appealing package. 'We're taking it market by market, to ensure that we respect the cultural variations within the Hispanic community,' said Round Hill General Manager Morgan Zaninovich. 'With the Bolsa de Recetas, we are expanding on our multi-pronged marketing program designed specifically to be culturally appropriate to Hispanic families.'[8]

Instead of creating a new wine specifically targeted at the Hispanic community, Round Hill Winery's approach is to make all their wines accessible to everybody, including the Hispanic community: 'Round Hill's strategy is to immerse itself into the culture, becoming part of the community and providing educational materials bilingually to reach a broader audience with integrity and ease of communication. We are not marketing to Hispanics, rather we are marketing as Hispanics,' said Marketing Director Fontes. 'Round Hill is taking that message directly to where the Hispanic customer shops with bilingual demonstrators at the store level. The demonstrators provide information about wine and food pairing with Latino cuisine, useful advice for selecting the proper wine for a meal, gathering or as a gift.'[9]

This strategy did pay off in the long term. Round Hill Winery, now Rutherford Ranch, was started in the late 1970s by Ernie and Virginia Van Asperen. Upon their retirement, long-time shareholders Marko and Theo Zaninovich acquired the winery. Today, Rutherford Wine Company includes four quality brands: Rutherford Ranch, Rutherford Ranch Reserve, Round Hill and Grand Pacific.

Vertical tribalism

Horizontal tribalism caters to specific groups, while vertical tribalism allows various groups to gather around a brand, a theme or a specific interest. That is why, for example, web sites around a specific topic, like wine or wine clubs, have so much importance and are so popular among wine drinkers. Wine consumers find in them a community which shares the same tastes, the same values and the same interests. It does not mean disagreements or controversies never happen among the tribe. It means the discussion can be civil and lively at the same time.

Tribalism is very important in retailing, which includes the wine business. Brands nurture tribes and pamper them. The customer loyalty is part of the tribalism. Buying a brand means belonging to a tribe. Let us take the example of the Pop Champagne created by Pommery in 1999, and developed by Nathalie Vranken after the acquisition of the Pommery House of Champagne in 2002.

Pop is an authentic Champagne created by the cellar master of Pommery, Thierry Gasco. First of all, there is a very specific technique that reduces the pressure in the bottle from 3.5 kgs to 1.2 kgs. This technique prevents all the bubbles reaching the nasal cavities of the drinker and provoking a sneeze. Second, all the qualities of the Champagne were preserved. It is made using the traditional Champagne method with a large proportion of Chardonnay. Last but not least, it is a beautifully designed object in a 250ml bottle, created in blue in 1999 and later in pink (for young women). It was then developed with various patterns and themes, thanks to the creative imagination of Nathalie Vranken.[10]

> Unconventional and impertinent, Pop is a champagne which is resolutely forward-looking, perfect for people who appreciate beauty and non-conformism and are in search of new sensations. Pop is the sound of the cork exploding from the bottle, conjuring up the euphoria and spontaneity of festive nights.[11]

Pop Champagne is distributed in wine stores as well as in night clubs. It is available in Paris, London, New York, Tokyo and wherever there are Champagne lovers. Who drinks Pop? Asked this question, Nathalie Vranken answered without a single second of hesitation: 'Everybody – absolutely everybody! Young people in night clubs, couples who want a celebration glass since there are exactly two glasses in a bottle, elderly women receiving a friend at home, people who love to drink a single glass before, with or after their meal, seniors, middle-aged, men and women. There is no specific demographic for Pop lovers.'

Why is this drink so popular among every category of people? Is it because people crave secure relationships and loyalty to a brand creates such a feeling? Is it a reaction against 'a uniform globalized world'? Maybe a little of all of those things, but it is also because Pop Champagne was able to create a personalized and emotional relationship with its customers. The Champagne 'people buy becomes the means to an end, and the end is a feeling,' explained marketing consultant Pamela Danziger in her book *Why People Buy Things They Don't Need*.[12]

Emotion and personalization of the relationship between the brand and the customer sustain the tribalism, and give the feeling of belonging to the tribe – a comforting feeling in a world very often felt to be menacing and violent.

U – as in universal

Universal or global? The two terms seem to be synonymous – universal being less depreciative than global. Universal can also be tribal. Pop Champagne is sold all over the world, but still is perceived as tribal. That is what Patrick Dixon calls 'future branding,' 'the reshaping of a brand not only for today's needs but also for tomorrow's globalization.'[13]

This is also why 'globalization forces corporations with strong tribal (national) identities to ask: who is us?'[14] This remark applies very well to the wine industry and the problem of regional branding. Can a wine brand rely only on its geographical area to be identified as a strong brand by potential customers? How is an American or a Japanese going to react to a Cahors wine? How will he react to a French Malbec? Here we are talking about the same wine – the Black wine of Cahors, the French Malbec.

In the United States, Argentine wines are very much identified as Malbec and Malbec is the variety on the rise among consumers. On August 27, 2007, the author of the famous wine blog Vinography.com, Alder Yarrow, wrote the story of his trip to Argentina:

> Once upon a time, I went to Argentina looking for good wine. Frankly I couldn't understand what all the fuss was about when it came to Malbec. Most of the ones I had tasted here in the Unites States were mediocre ... Scratching my head, I traipsed off to Argentina looking for the promised land. Or promised bottle, as the case may be. And I found it. We had a lot of great Malbec while we were there, and really got a chance to appreciate the Argentinean skill at high altitude viticulture.

He became enthralled by the Bodegas Colomé wines in Salta:

> Bodegas Colomé now farms some of the oldest vines in Argentina. Significantly younger than 16th century, but 150-year-old pre-phylloxera, own-rooted Malbec and Cabernet vines are nothing to sneeze at. The estate's

250 acres of vines from old French cuttings also hold the claim of being some of the highest altitude vineyards in the world, with the highest being a staggering 9891 feet above sea level.

To sum up Alder Yarrow's rave about Colomé, it is biodynamically farmed, low yield, hand-sorted, cold-soaked, new barrel-aged, grown at an altitude of over 2500 meters and sold for $30 a bottle, which is cheap for a great wine on the American market, but expensive for an Argentinian one, since, as he pointed out earlier, the Argentinian Malbecs available on the US market are usually cheap.

In the imagination of some American consumers, Malbec is a mediocre wine from Argentina. In the imagination of some others, Malbec is a beautiful grape giving birth, with the help of talented winemakers, to beautiful wines. Now the Malbec producers from France, mostly located in the Cahors region, are conducting a campaign to market their wines in the United States as 'the French Malbec,' the 'Black wine of Cahors.' Here is one of the ambiguities of the universal (or global) trend. We have the same grape – Malbec – coming from two geographical areas, the famous Argentina and the unknown Cahors, a small city in the South-West of France. Is it really in the best interest of Cahors to be associated with Argentina, at the risk of confusing the consumer? Globalization for the consumer may mean confusion.

On the other hand, consumers are traveling more and more, becoming aware of other wines and other countries. By giving a very strong identity to a brand like Malbec and differentiating it very clearly from its Argentinian counterpart, Cahors will be clearly identified as the French Malbec.

Yellow Tail is now identified as THE Australian brand, marketing in the United States approximately ten varietal wines, like Chardonnay, Shiraz, Merlot, Cabernet, even Riesling, and it is now the number one brand sold in the US!

Whether it is Malbec from France or Argentina, Cabernet Sauvignon from Bordeaux or California, Syrah or Shiraz from France, California or Australia, universal – which denies regional branding – is the antithesis of radical.

R – as in radical

Radical as in 'going back to your roots' or radical as in 'politically radical' are the two choices that can be made. Patrick Dixon chose the second road: 'The future will have a strong radical element to it, as traditional political movements shrivel and die. The digital revolution created the global village and globalization the rules for trading within it, but neither has taught us how several billion people should live inside such a tiny cultural space.'[15]

The 'tiny cultural space' is not that tiny as we see it. It looks more like various bubbles close to each other with fragmented knowledge or interest. For example, the wine community is a vast bubble with smaller bubbles inside it, or next to it. The Champagne lovers, the Chardonnay amateurs, the old wines lovers, the New World wines buffs or the Bordeaux fans, all those cultural bubbles are forming a giant single bubble all over the world.

That is why we think the first road is more appropriate to the wine business. Studies show that young people interested in wine want to go back to the roots of the industry. Maybe the regional branding will be up-to-date in future years. Wine lovers in general expect less marketing and a more human-related emphasis from the industry. They want to put a face and a story behind the wine.

Is that why so many wine drinkers love to read the family history of a wine business? Even the most contemporary of wineries, like the Casella winery, creator of the Australian Yellow Tail brand, boasts on its web site about its family history since 1820. Under the romantic title, 'Casella Family Heritage,' they write that 'The Casella family has been making wine since 1820 – first in Italy and since 1965 in Australia. Filippo and Maria Casella emigrated to Australia from Italy in the 1950s bringing with them their hopes and dreams and the know-how acquired through three generations of grape-growing and winemaking in Italy.' After telling the story up to today, the web site concludes with 'Today Casella Wines is run by Filippo's three sons – John, Managing Director and Winemaker; Joe, Australian Sales Director; and Marcello, Director and Vineyard Manager. Filippo's grandchildren – Philip and Rachelle – are the sixth generation to join the business.' The story acts to give a wine business its legitimacy and allows it to 'compete' with the 400 or 500-year old European wine properties.

E – as in ethical

This story of a wine and its makers can also help a business to face some of the single issues, such as contemporary concerns about the environment or the organic growing of the grapes. That is where tribal meets radical meets ethical. Corporate ethics are very important in the modern world and can justify cause-related marketing.

'The final face of the future is ethical,' claims Patrick Dixon.[16] In a world where environmental issues, economics and society are global, ethics are going to be the real value which corporations, people and governments are going to need. The wine business is no exception. Consumers are expecting ethical conduct from the winemakers, respect for the law in drinking politics, as well as environmentally safe management of the vineyard.

Case Study: pink wines and pink ribbon

In the same way as the red ribbon is the symbol for the fight against AIDS, the pink ribbon symbolizes the fight against breast cancer. The association of the color pink with some of their wines – the 'rosato wine' from Italy, the 'rosé wine' from France or the 'pink wine' of America – encouraged some winemakers to donate part of their profits to, say, a research center, or to organize a tasting whose profits would go to this cause. The list of such wineries is very long, mostly in California where cause-related marketing is very common. Since 2000, Chrystal Clifton, co-owner with her husband, of the Palmina winery, has organized a campaign called 'Pink Wine for the Pink Ribbon.' Each year, a portion of the price of her Botasea pink wine is donated to a research center on breast cancer.

In May 2007, Manuel Ferreira, the owner of the restaurant Le Gavroche in Vancouver, hosted a four-course 'Think Pink' Rosé wine and food pairing dinner throughout the month of May. He said the concept for the fundraiser ($5 from every Think Pink dinner is donated to the British Columbia Cancer Foundation in support of breast cancer research and awareness) began when his best friend died of breast cancer. This initiative requires some courage on the part of a restaurant owner because of the poor image of pink wines in consumers' minds, as blog authors, Susan M Boyce and Frank Haddad, wrote in their blog blanc-de-noir.com:

> The result is the first of what Manuel anticipates will become an annual tradition at Le Gavroche – a pairing of 'pink' wines with inspired culinary creations. From an oenophile's point of view, his decision is not only a bold departure from tradition but a challenge few would be willing to risk. Eliminating both red and white wines effectively removes more than 95 percent of possible pairings – and virtually all 'classic' matches. Add in the unfortunately still lingering public perception of Rosé wines as

sweet, cloying, cheap plonk, and it's astonishing anyone would even attempt it. To pull it off with aplomb is a credit to Manuel's expertise and tenacity.[17]

Whatever their reservations about the wine list, Susan and Frank were happy to contribute 'in some very small way to improving the hope of a cure for cancer.'

'Think before you pink'

Associating with a good cause does not always ensure success when the intention is not 100 percent genuine and sincere. Sutter Home Wines, one of the brands of the Trinchero Family Estates in California, launched a campaign on 'Breast Cancer Awareness' by putting a pink ribbon on each of its White Zinfandel bottles. 'We believe this will communicate a message of hope and remind women to take a moment for themselves and schedule a mammogram or exam,' said the management. The Marin Institute, established in Marin County, California, whose goals are to alert the Marin population to the dangers of alcohol, immediately stigmatized the Sutter Home initiative in their feature 'What they don't tell you': 'Alcohol is a known human carcinogen, and drinking it is a risk factor for developing breast cancer. Women who have two to five drinks a day have about 1.5 times the risk of women who drink no alcohol.'[18] By doing so the Marin Institute is relaying the campaign at the centre of a project of Breast Cancer Action (BCA), 'Think before you pink.' Breast Cancer Action and its campaign 'Think Before You Pink' was launched in 2002 in response to growing concern about the overwhelming number of pink-ribbon products and promotions on the market. The campaign calls for more transparency and accountability by companies that take part in breast cancer fundraising, and encourages consumers to ask critical questions about pink-ribbon promotions. 'Think Before You Pink also highlights "pinkwashers" – companies that purport to care about breast cancer by promoting a pink-ribbon campaign, but manufacture products that are linked to the disease.' BCA calls attention to the car industry, some cosmetics companies and any industry having a negative impact on women's health, and dubs them the 'pinkwashers.' They ask women to be aware of those companies and to take action against them.

Indeed, there is abundant evidence that 'the final face of the future is ethical,' as Dr. Dixon said.

Measuring the future of the wine business?

At the end of his book, Patrick Dixon defines a way for businesses to measure their future. Can we do the same with the wine business? Let us try!

The basic grid as imagined by Dixon is two equal halves of a wheel as illustrated in Figure 2.1.

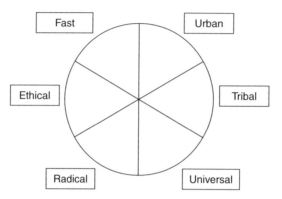

Figure 2.1   A basic Dixon measuring grid

Dixon's instructions are: 'The technique is simple and fast: mark on each of the six lines how strong you think your organization is in the six key areas … When the points are joined up you get a unique shape.'

Of course it is very subjective, but it shows how you see your future. Do you want to try for your business or the wine industry? Just let us know …!

CHAPTER 3

Birth of the new wine consumer

In Mumbai, our new Indian wine drinker, Mr. Singh, is sitting in a restaurant with a friend who orders wine with his dinner. 'Red or white?,' asks the waiter. 'Red with ice and soda,' answers Mr. Singh's friend. How embarrassing!

In Beijing, our Chinese wine drinker, Li, sips a glass of Yongning wine, from the rising Chinese wine area. The imported wines are so expensive he does not think he can afford them.

In Moscow, Natasha hesitates between a glass of Georgian wine traditionally available in Russia, and rather cheap, and a glass of imported, and very costly, Bordeaux Classified growth – impressing her friends.

Worldwide, wine consumption patterns are changing. Indeed, with the world changing so dramatically because of new technologies and the increasing economical power of emerging countries, wine drinkers have had little choice but to adapt their behavioral patterns to the new circumstances. New consumers, including women and young people, are coming to the fore. There are also whole new groups of customers from emerging markets such as India, Russia and China.

Whether in traditional markets like the Western countries and Japan or in emerging markets, the difference lies in the way wine is consumed. The trends towards new consuming habits makes the way wine is drunk different from the 'old days.'

Many market studies proposed an interesting segmentation of end-consumers in several countries. Based on their geographical approach to the profiles of consumers, we will provide a cross-cultural portrait of the wine consumer – a kind of instant global picture.

The traditional markets

The traditional markets cover most of the Western world, Europe and North America, as well as Japan. Many European countries are wine producers, such as France, Germany, Italy, Spain, Portugal and Greece. The others usually import their wines from those countries, with various degrees of importance.

The new wine consumer in Europe

Wine consumption in Europe is changing drastically. The wine-producing countries – particularly France, Spain, Portugal and Italy – are experiencing a decline in consumption, while in Northern European countries consumption is clearly rising, as shown in Table 3.1.

In the countries traditionally producing wine, wine was considered as food and part of the daily diet for many years. Now, wine is becoming

Table 3.1 Typology of wine consumption in Europe by country (in liters of wine per person per year)

Country	1961	1970	1980	1990	2001	2006
Producers; high levels of production; high levels of consumption, falling						
France	126.1	109.1	91	72.7	53.9	
Greece	41	40	44.9	32.8	34	
Italy	108.2	113.7	92.9	62.5	50	48
Portugal	99.3	9.9	68.7	63.3	50	41
Spain	52.5	61.5	64.7	37.4	36.2	28
Producers; moderate consumption, stagnating or increasing slightly						
Austria	20.8	34.6	35.8	35	31	
Czech Rep.	12.4	14.6	15.5	14.8	16.5	17
Germany	12.2	16	25.5	26.1	23.9	25
Switzerland	36.7	41.9	47.4	49.4	43.1	38
Not producers; continuous rise in consumption						
Belgium	8.6	14.2	20.6	24.9	18.7	23
Denmark	3.3	5.9	14	21.3	31.2	32
Finland	1.3	3	4.7	6.4	20.1	29
Netherlands	2.3	5.2	12.9	14.5	18.9	21
Norway	1.3	2.3	4.4	6.4	11	13
Sweden	3.6	6.4	9.5	12.3	15.5	17
UK	1.8	2.9	7.1	11.5	17.5	17

Source: Focus, issue no. 6, 2003, p. 16.

an 'occasional' drink for celebration and/or social occasions, such as dinner with friends and business meals.

An opposing trend, that is a switch to wine, can be seen to be developing in countries where beer is usually drunk and, similarly, in countries such as Scandinavia where spirits are traditionally drunk.

What do the wine consumers drink?

Even if there are changes in the way people drink in every country, they still have a limited choice between red, rosé and white wines. Analyzing such information gives us a good idea about what they like.

From the study published in the n.6 issue of *Focus* in 2003, we can deduce that there are two categories of multinational wine consumer:

- **New wine consumers**, who have traditionally drunk beer and spirits rather than wine, come from countries such as the United States, Japan, the Netherlands, Norway, Sweden, Finland, Poland, Russia, the Czech Republic, Singapore, Hong Kong, China and India, as Table 3.2 shows below.
- **Traditional wine consumers**, who come from traditionally wine drinking countries, such as France, Belgium, Germany, Luxembourg, Switzerland, Spain, Portugal, Italy and Austria, as shown in Table 3.3 on next page.

Table 3.2   The new consumer (2007)

Country	Consumption (l/hab/yr)	Red wines %	Rosé wines %	White wines %
USA	8	41	19	40
Singapore	2	65	2	33
Hong Kong	2	60	10	30
Japan	3	48	8	43
Norway	13	73	1	23
UK	17	50	3	47
Sweden	17	61	3	36
Finland	29	49	1	50
Poland	5	56	1	43
Russia	6	70	0	30
Czech Rep.	17	40	0	60
China	1	80	2	18
India	1			40

Source: septimanie-export.com/fr/tendances, 2007.

Table 3.3   The traditional consumer (2007)

Country	Consumption	Red wines %	Rosés wines %	White wines %
Belgium	23	58	14	28
Germany	25	53	7	40
Luxemburg	64	Nc	Nc	53
Switzerland	38	69	0	31
Denmark	32	70	3	27
Spain	28	55	17	28
Portugal	41	75	0	25
Italy	48	55	7	37
Netherlands	21	61	9	30
Austria	29	44	0	56

Source: septimanie-export.com/fr/tendances, 2007.

The emerging markets: China, Russia and India

In these countries, wine is not the first choice of drink, as we saw in the previous chapter, and is mostly an acquired taste. In 2005 for the first time, China and Russia entered the top ten among wine-consuming countries – China being number 10 and Russia number 8. India is on the road to joining them, with wine sales increasing by 34 percent each year.

But figures will not give us an answer to the main questions. How are people drinking in those countries? What are they drinking? Why are they drinking? Who are the drinkers? However, because no in-depth, comprehensive study has ever been conducted in any of these countries, the marketers have to read local studies available in English, or rely on information scattered throughout the Internet. In spite of these difficulties, it is possible to draw a fairly accurate image of the emerging markets.

India: fiery food and delicate wines?

As pointed out in Chapter 2, Indian food can be rather spicy, even fiery, which means it is not very wine friendly. Is that why wine is usually drunk away from home and not with food? Indians adopted the British habit of having a strong drink – usually a glass of Scotch whisky – before dinner. This being so they are used to having and enjoying a drink before their meals, so why not a glass of wine? And this is what is happening, wine has become the new fashionable drink among young urbanites. The most popular wines are Cabernet Sauvignon, one of the grapes blended in the Bordeaux wines, and the Indian Cabernet Sauvignon and Syrah blend from the Nandi Hills in Southern India.

To learn more and avoid the embarrassment of a *faux-pas*, young executives in international corporations learn about wine through wine tastings and classes. Mr. Singh is educating himself because he knows it is important to impress colleagues and clients when at a corporate dinner.

The situation is more delicate for Indian women. Alcohol drinking still remains taboo for most women in India. This is no longer absolutely true in major cities, however, where young professional women represent a significant segment of the wine market.

Yet the wine business is largely male dominated. The first Indian woman ever to enter a course to become a sommelier is Ashwini Awate, admitted to the International Masters Vintage in Vine and Wine Management program at the Ecole Supérieure d'Agriculture (ESA) at Angers in France. This was under the Erasmus Scholarship program awarded by the European Union (EU) to non-European students wishing to pursue higher education in the EU. Ashwini Awate recognizes the need for local experts in the Indian wine industry to select wines for stores, organize events and sell wines. Awate's goal is to start her own all-women wine enterprise. 'This will be like a women's co-operative,' she told the author of the blog Sommelier India, 'comprising mostly friends who will pool in their talents and expertise from various fields including marketing and exports.' She also plans to launch a web site to make information on the wine industry available.

In the interim, what would prevent an Indian from drinking good wines? Two things: ignorance and a fear of mispronouncing foreign names. A young woman, with a good knowledge of wine, reported that her own wine retailer advised her to buy 'kotay dou Ronnie,' meaning 'Côtes du Rhône.' Is that so shameful? After all, a South African wine-maker had no scruple about naming his own wine 'Goats Do Roam,' a play on the sound of the words!

For Indians – as a wine drinker confessed to journalist Amrit Dhillon of the *Sunday Telegraph*: 'Drinking wine confers a badge of sophistication. It's got great snob value.'[1]

China and wine: a recent love story

The same 'snob value' applies to Russian and Chinese wine drinkers. Indeed, the drinkers' profiles are the same: rich people, executives, high-ranking officials and new millionaires. They drink expensive imported wines, while middle-class people drink local wines, but everyone wants to drink wine. It is a matter of social status and image. In Beijing and in Shanghai, wine is the gift that will give most pleasure and prestige, especially imported French wines.

Wine is still a mystery to most Chinese. The average wine consumer in China is between 20 and 35 years old, relatively affluent and living in an urban area. Chinese consumers do not necessarily serve wine in the Western way. Iced red wine is popular – white wine is often mixed with coca-colas and red with sweet drinks. But, as in India, education is provided by tastings in stores, with more traveling and studying overseas creating an elite of connoisseurs.

Chinese wine experts believe that the market is made up of about 1,000,000 consumers with a potential of 30 million. Increasing numbers of international managers and executives study abroad and discover wine while traveling in Europe. Back in China, they retain their interest in wine and broaden their knowledge. They are mostly interested in red because of the symbolism of the color in Chinese culture. Red is associated with luck, happiness and wealth. White is the color of mourning and death, which influences against white wine. It also uses the same word used for liquors and rice wine – 'Bai Ju.' White wine, therefore, has a problem distinguishing itself from rice wine.

As in India, the language is a problem. Some wine names are very easy to remember: La Tour is 'La Tu' and Lafite 'La fei.' Some names are so complicated that people are afraid to order them: 'It's embarrassing to ask for a good wine when its name cannot be understood by my friends because of its pronunciation,' said a Chinese executive to *L'Amateur/The Wine Lovers* journalist, Sophie Liu (Fall 2007).

But the 'snob value' may be even higher in China than in India. It is a signal honor to be invited home by a VIP or official to sample a great bottle of wine, preferably one not yet available on the Chinese market and brought back from Europe. French wine is the favorite of all Chinese wine connoisseurs.

Russia: a sweet tooth but a sharp business class

The picture is almost identical in Russia. Drinking wine is a sign of status and social success. There are now a few hundred millionaires in Russia: their combined fortune is estimated at around $3.4 billion dollars. The richest of all is Roman Abramovich, whose fortune is estimated at $19.2 billion. The income of all Russians, however, has also increased. The average income of the middle class is now $7000 (around 4.800 euros) a year, while the national average is around $2,610 (about 1.800 euros) a year. Twenty million people are now living above the poverty level.

In this prosperous economy, more and more people have some disposable income. Wine is seen as a good way to spend that money; it is new and trendy as well as a sign of success. Russians drink mostly red wine (70 percent); white wine accounts for about 25 percent and rosé wines for the rest. Russians – a little like their American counterparts – have a sweet tooth. They love off-dry and semi-sweet flavors, even in red wines, with dry wines mostly reflecting the more sophisticated tastes and drinking habits of wealthy consumers. Young entrepreneurs and senior executives of international corporations are the main clients of the fine wine business. The wealthier wine consumers thrive on First Growth Bordeaux and cult wines from the New World.

The average wine drinker will mostly buy imported wines, such as those from Moldova (before the ban), Bulgaria, Georgia and France, with Italy now getting into the picture. The price of a bottle will be in the 3 euros range. In the major cities, like Moscow, St. Petersburg or Kiev, drinkers have much greater disposable incomes and spend more on premium wines.

The new wine drinkers of China, India and Russia have a common profile. More traveled, highly educated, with a high income, these drinkers have the time and the will to learn more about wine. They want access to the status symbols of the Western world. Wine, like luxury products, is highly desirable for these new consumers.

Europe, the United States and Japan: new wine drinkers and new consuming trends

Because wine is really part of the history of Europe, the United States and Japan, we are facing a different evolution. First of all, those countries have seen the birth of new wine drinkers: women and young people. Second, the consuming trends are changing: drinkers are now 'at-homers,' adventurous connoisseurs, weekly treaters, bargain hunters (or savvy shoppers), conservatives (or traditionalists), enthusiasts, image seekers or 'natives.' These trends are cross-cultural and affect almost every country.

New wine drinkers

Bridget Jones prefers Chardonnay

As we saw in the previous chapter, wine was a man's world for many years, both personally and professionally. The last years of the twentieth century saw the emergence of women as consumers and professionals in the wine business. How did it happen? Who are the women who drink wine? How do they buy and consume wine? Will their new consuming trends affect the wine industry positively or negatively? These are all questions that need an answer.

Women are usually in charge of the grocery shopping and, consequently, frequently buy the wine; 70 percent to 80 percent of wines are bought by women. In the United Kingdom, according to the Mintel study conducted in 2005, more than 60 percent of British wine drinkers are women; among those, seven out of ten drink wine at least once a month. The average woman drinker is professionally active, aged between 30 and 40, loves Chardonnay and buys wine mostly during sales. That is why this type of British wine drinker is described as being of the 'Bridget Jones generation.'

Women and wine: wine divas, not wine geeks

Other studies, however, show that women are not as comfortable as men in choosing and buying a bottle of wine, because they feel they do not know enough about it. That is why they rely on bargains, advertising, labels and word of mouth. They also buy differently from men. They buy a bottle to celebrate an event, for a special dinner, as a gift or to share with their women friends. In California during the summer in 2007, I was looking at various wine brands and noticed a pink wine with a pink label simply called ... 'Bitch'! A little surprised, I asked the manager of the wine department how this wine was selling. 'Very well,' he answered. 'It's one of our best sellers. It's mostly bought by women who are going to meet with their girl friends for an evening of fun.' Maybe, because I am European, I think I would feel a little embarrassed giving one of my friends a wine labeled 'Bitch'!

A study conducted by the Wine Intelligence Group in 2006 tracked the difference between the wine consuming habits of men and women (Table 3.4). It was conducted on a base of 1300 regular wine consumers in the United Kingdom.

Table 3.4 The wine consuming habits of men and women (percentage difference)

Question	Men	Women
Highly interested in wine	21%	11%
Moderately interested in wine	58%	57%
Very little interested in wine	21%	32%
More likely to buy a bottle between £3–£3.99	28%	38%
More likely to buy a bottle between £4–£4.99	26%	31%
More likely to buy a bottle between £5–5.99	20%	12%
Like opening a bottle with a screw cap	24%	37%
Like opening a bottle with a synthetic cork	64%	49%
Like opening a bottle with a natural cork	37%	32%
Like buying a bottle with a screw cap	23%	27%
Like buying a bottle with a synthetic cork	19%	22%
Like buying a bottle with a natural cork	56%	55%

This summary of the Wine Intelligence Group study shows that:

• women are interested in wine but less passionately than men;
• women are less likely to treat themselves to an expensive bottle;
• women are less traditional than men in their way of drinking: they accept less traditional closures more readily than men do – possibly for practical reasons. Unscrewing a cap is much easier than uncorking a bottle, and does not require a specific tool (which you can forget when going on a picnic, for example).

What does this tell us about women and wine? Wine is a lifestyle, not a subject of study or erudition. The same Wine Intelligence Group study tells us there are two favorite moments for women in wine drinking:

- Women's 'self' wine drinking moment: it is their moment of relaxation and freedom, the moment of the day or the week that belongs only to them.
- Women's 'sociable' wine drinking moment: they connect with their friends or family, they share joy, pleasure and conviviality.

'Women are the future of wine' in the United States

In the United States, women buy more than 70 percent of the wines and drink about 60 percent. They buy supermarket brands, of course, but also premium wines (costing $15 and more). The wine industry is so convinced that 'women are the future of wine,' according to the title of the convention held in Bordeaux in 2006, that many producers tailor wine to the tastes of women. What are they? Women are thought to enjoy wines which are fruity, lighter in color and lower in alcohol. These so-called 'feminine' wines hit the shelves in the United States in 2006: 'Flower Label' by Georges Duboeuf; 'White Lie Early Season,' a Chardonnay with fewer calories and a 9.8 percent alcohol content, by Beringer Blass, a subsidiary of the Australian group Fosters; as well as 'Grand Embrace' and 'Mad Housewife' by Rainier Wines, a merchant in Seattle. At the same time, a wine magazine specifically dedicated to women wine drinkers, *Wine Adventure*, was launched. These wines, as well as the magazine seem, however, to have died from a lack of oxygen – I mean, interest.

Even if wine is supposed to be fun and relaxing, buying a bottle is a serious decision because it is costly and status-related. A consumer – especially a woman – cannot afford to make a mistake, because the wrong buy can ruin an evening. As Leslie Sbrocco, Christine Ansbacher, Natalie Maclean and other female authors on wine have pointed out, women are more about 'we than me.' Wine is part of a social event, and must contribute to its success. Women look for the right Italian wine for their new Italian dish or the perfect Australian Shiraz for their kangaroo steaks, rather than basing their decisions on vintage charts or ratings.

In wine advertising, women connect more easily with people sharing a good time, glass in hand, than with the image of a bottle featured in the center of the picture. This is what Gina Gallo and Sofia Coppola grasped when they put themselves or their family at the heart of their ads or on their website. Why is that? It is because women connect emotionally more easily than men, and that is why American advertisers feature more and more women-only gatherings in their wine ads and web sites. The Sutter Home Winery book club features three women having a good time together a glass of wine in hand. On the St. Supery website, a silhouetted woman with glass in hand is facing a silhouetted man. On the Mondavi site, women are featured in many of their events.

Japanese female wine drinkers

Similar behavior seems to apply to Japanese women as well. In Japan, women's consumption of wine is increasing: 42.3 percent drink wine at least once a week, 6.1 percent drink it every day. Until very recently, Japanese women could not have a career of their own and be independent. Nowadays more and more young women work and are single. Those young working women are the future of the wine business in Japan. 'Yes, a few men are spending huge sums on Grand Cru and Parker-point wines,' writes Sandra Shoji in *Wines and Vines* (November 2004), 'but most Japanese men are quite happy to sip beer, sake and shochu over comfort food of curry rice or grilled fish in inexpensive restaurants. It is the women who are out there daily in the trenches of fusion, European and Southeast Asian restaurants, pondering if New World Riesling is the right match for Vietnamese pho or pumpkin risotto.'

Like their European and American counterparts, they enjoy wine after work as a social moment as well as its potential for enhancing their elegant and refined food. They usually drink outside home in a wine bar or at a tasting in a wine store. Their mothers are also the new wine drinkers: free from parenting duties and not working, those women travel, discover wine while abroad and come back home to learn about and buy wine, especially French wine in restaurants and wine stores.

They are helped in their quest for knowledge and pleasure by the powerful Japanese Association of Sommeliers, whose younger members are not as locked into French wines as their elders and are more open to New World wines. They clear space on their store shelves for wines more friendly to Japanese food and more appealing to women. 'While traditional import managers shudder at the idea of sparkling and sweet wines, Japanese women are stamping their stiletto heels, demanding bubbly for aperitifs and dessert wines for after dinner, with chocolate,' explains journalist Sandra Shoji.

For an American, European or Japanese woman, drinking a glass of wine is a moment of pleasure, not the occasion to talk about tannins, acidity or vintage: it tastes good, it feels good. Women are not wine geeks, they are wine divas!

Young people: the other newcomers in wine drinking

Younger people, both Millennials and GenXers, are the particular favorites of marketers and the wine industry. New to wine in the United States and in Japan, they love to experiment, they travel more extensively than their elders, very often to Europe and its wine-producing countries, and have a good disposable income. In the United States, they account for about 70 million people (26 percent), second only to the baby boomer generation (77 million). More interestingly, the percentage of Millennials who consume wine has increased from 10 percent in 2004 to 17 percent in 2006. Even more interesting, Millennials and GenXers are more inclined to drink wine than beer.

How did they become interested in wine? For some of them, their parents drank wine and they grew up with wine on the table. 'My parents are both big into wine,' said 22-year-old Jennifer Hammons to journalist Deborah Pankey, *Daily Herald* Food Editor on November 30, 2005. 'At first I didn't like it, but then it grew on me.' There is much the same scenario for young people in France: wine is a food always on the family table. Young children are encouraged to taste a drop of champagne or wine during family gatherings. Later in their teens, they are given a third of a glass of wine or champagne with their meal. Why do they then reject wine to go on to choosing beer, cocktails or liquors? Very often, as sociologist Céline Simonnet-Toussaint explains in her book *Le Vin sur le Divan*, young people under 25 reject wine because it is the symbol of the family. Young people want to experiment with their freedom, but they come back to wine at around 25, when they get their first job, their first 'real' apartment and start settling into their new life.

Others discover wine by themselves – perhaps during a trip to a wine country, like Napa in the United States, Burgundy in France, Tuscany in

Italy, Priorato in Spain or Porto in Portugal. They get interested, go to wine classes or tastings, join a wine club and explore wine stores to get good advice. Mostly, like the women, they listen to their peers, surf the Internet to read about wine and discuss their new passion in forums.

Wines to suit the 'coca cola generation'?

The wine industry is aware of the need of young people for more knowledge. At the same time, this new generation of wine drinkers is very different from preceding generations. It is the 'coca cola generation': they have a much sweeter tooth, they are 'zappers,' having known TV and the Internet all their lives, and they are used to getting what they want and paying a high price for it. After all, they pay $3.50 for their daily Starbucks cappuccino and download their songs for $1 or their movies for $5 every day on their iPod or MP3. They know that everything has a price and usually a high price.

Taking these parameters into account, some winemakers considered designing wines specifically targeted at Millennials and GenXers: fun labels, fruit-forward wines and a high price. Millennials do not hesitate to pay up to $20 for a bottle of wine! Indeed, they do not as yet have any heavy financial burdens: no children, often a two-income household, no parents to take care of, a good salary and a large disposable income. Unfortunately for the wine industry, they rarely buy the same bottle twice, because there is such a huge choice of brands. They want to be the first to discover a new brand or a new trend, the first to try them and share them with their peers.

Nonetheless, major groups have designed brands for Millennials as they have for women. Constellation designed 3 Blind Moose, Four Emus, Monkey Bay and other 'fun' brands. There is no talk of *terroir* or wine-making on the packaging. The label does not tell a wine story, but a story of having a good time and fun with your friends. These brands sell well. Gary Glass, former Vice-President of Marketing for Constellation's Centerra Wine Company, estimates that 3 Blind Moose sold 175,000 cases in 18 months on the market.

A similar strategy was launched by pioneering entrepreneur Richard Branson, who founded Virgin Wines in 2005. Branson did not create new brands but marketed existing brands in a fun and different way. On the homepage of the site, there is a little sexual joke addressed to younger wine drinkers.

Figure 3.1   Screen capture: Virgin Wines
Source: Virgin Wines.

If the young people are 'nervous about their first time' (Figure 3.1), they will get free delivery of a case of wines at half price. Is this deal not the best encouragement to order one can think of?

At the same time, young people are not as comfortable as their elders when they buy wine. They can be adventurous, but they also seek quality and certainty. Whether they are American, European or Japanese, they will rely on a classic wine from Europe or a well-known luxury brand from the New World. Wine is still a little intimidating for Millennials.

Women and young people: the new faces of the wine industry

Women and young people are the new faces courted by the wine industry and winemakers. They do not seem to mind being directly marketed and targeted by the wine industry. They are not turned off by big brands, as older wine drinkers frequently are. In fact, women and Millennials follow the trends. Fruit-forward wines are the trend, in the same way white Zinfandel was popular in the 1980s and Chardonnay in the 1990s. Wine styles evolve, following the taste of the new wine drinkers. But women and Millennials are going to evolve too, and, as they become more experienced and more knowledgeable about wine, their level of sophistication is also going to rise.

New consuming trends

Indeed, the new wine consumers, young or mature, men or women, change and become more sophisticated. They then join the core of other wine drinkers. Is it possible to identify a typology of wine drinkers in the traditional markets – some trans-cultural trends?

Several studies, conducted in Europe, the United States and the United Kingdom over the last two years,[2] clearly showed several common trends among American, European and British wine consumers. These studies were conducted among core or marginal wine drinkers in their respective countries. The differences are all quite subtle.

Enthusiasts, at-homers and satisfied sippers

Called 'enthusiasts' and 'satisfied sippers' in the United States and 'at-homers' in the United Kingdom, this category of wine drinkers constitutes the majority – about 40 percent of wine drinkers. They are very much involved in wine, learning as much as they can and sharing their discoveries with families and friends. While their involvement is high, their budget might not be very substantial. Their spending is average (about $5–8 or £4–5 per bottle) and they prefer to drink at home rather than in restaurants. They are usually middle-class suburban professionals aged 35–50 with a family.

Adventurous connoisseurs and image seekers

These two categories have a lot in common. They both have a high income, are heavily involved in wine drinking and buying and are sophisticated drinkers. They drink all types of wine from both the New World and the Old World. The image seekers are more sensitive to the social image that a prestigious and expensive wine or a fun label can bring to their status.

This is a rising trend in Europe. Little by little, the continental European market is opening to wines from outside Europe: Chile, Argentina, California, Australia, South Africa, New Zealand. At first, only the most expensive wines of those countries were available in up-market wine stores, such as Lavinia in Paris, Barcelona, Madrid and Moscow. In the last few months, more popular wine chains, such as Nicolas in France, have introduced wines from several New World countries at an average price of 5–8 euros – the average spending of a French wine drinker. Major stores, such as Trader Joe's or Lazy Acres in America and Tesco in the United Kingdom, promote wines from other countries and try to educate their consumers. Bringing wines like these to a dinner party or serving them to one's friends flatters one's image as an adventurous connoisseur.

Sociable promotion-seekers, bargain hunters or savvy shoppers

Whatever the name, this category is composed of frequent buyers who are motivated by bargain offers. They are not connoisseurs, but enjoy wine at least three times a week. Savvy shoppers might be on the look-out for great wines at a great price, but they do not believe a wine has to cost a lot to be good. Bargain hunters will buy wine based on a budget and with a good price-quality ratio.

Standing in the aisle of the wine department of an American super-market, I saw a middle-aged woman pushing her cart in a very resolute way along the shelves. I was looking for a wine and was indecisive. On the other hand, she looked like somebody who knew what she wanted to buy. I saw her walking with no hesitation to the Australian wine section and put in her cart three bottles of Yellow Tail. 'Why did you choose those wines over so many?,' I asked her. She looked at me a little puzzled: 'They're very good wines, usually cheap and now they're even on sale. It's a great bargain!' 'Why three bottles?.' She said she had a party that night at home, and, since she knew those wines were good, her friends would not be disappointed.

This woman is very representative of the savvy shopper who recognizes a good wine when she sees one.

It does not mean they cannot be adventurous by buying out-of-the-ordinary wines or lesser-known bottles. As Bob Wesley, wine manager of the Lazy Acres Market in Santa Barbara explained to me, wine stores have an educational role to play towards wine consumers (Figure 3.2 on next page). That is why he very often puts on sale good quality wines to encourage his clients to try them. They get in at the budget level acceptable to bargain hunters, who will become adventurous – if the price is right.

Figure 3.2   Bob Wesley of Lazy Acres, Santa Barbara
Source: Resmo.

Traditionalists and weekly treaters

This category is by far the largest; it includes any aspiring wine drinker. They feel concerned by their lack of knowledge, which sometimes leads them to a more 'traditional' choice, either a bottle from the Old World with a classical label or, on the other hand, one with a fun label.

The traditionalists are more inclined to buy a well-known brand at a reasonable price, while the weekly treaters might spend more to make sure they have a good bottle.

The international overwhelmed consumer

The overwhelmed consumer stands in the aisle of the supermarket trying to choose a wine for dinner, a special occasion or as a gift. He might not go into an independent wine store out of sheer shyness or fear of sounding ignorant. The overwhelmed consumer can be anyone – young, old, female, male, suburban, urban or rural.

Every country has to deal with the overwhelmed consumer. This is the category that is most interesting for the wine industry. It means, indeed, that there is a gap, that the industry does not satisfy the needs of potential consumers.

How can the industry answer this need? There are, of course, traditional means, such as shelf talkers, information on the back label or press advertising. There are also more contemporary ways of dealing with the problem, such as an informative web site, webcasts, blogs which have been created through Web 1.0 and Web 2.0 on the Internet.

PART II

Reaching the new consumer

CHAPTER 4

Traditional marketing versus web marketing

Marketing wine is a New World concept. The Old World overlooks marketing strategy. As Don and Petie Kladstrup pointed out in their book *Wine and War*, until World War II most winemakers in Europe felt that the only thing they had to do was make wine, and that people would come to buy it. Advertising and marketing were things they did not think they had to do. Many, in fact, felt it was beneath them. Today, they know their survival depends a lot on marketing and advertising, but they are still not very good at it, while the New World wineries are marketing champions.

In the difficult context of the wine industry, as well as in a very competitive environment, marketing has to be very well thought out and efficient. How and to whom should a wine or a brand be marketed? There are several options open to a winery: it might want to be different, segment or expand its market, create more value-added, communicate in a new way or build a new development model, such as a wine club.

The difference a good marketing strategy makes

The black wine of Cahors

The existence of the 'black wine' goes a long way back in history. Why black? Technically speaking the Cahors wines are red, but their color is almost black when the bottle is held to the light (see Figure 4.1). Planted by the Roman Emperors more than 2000 years ago, the Cahors vineyard has had a very turbulent history. Destroyed several times over the centuries, it was always replanted. In the Middle Ages, Cahors wines were renowned throughout Europe. Peter the Great, Tsar of Russia, Pope John XXII, bishops and kings loved the dark, strong wine. In

Figure 4.1   Black wine of Cahors
Source: Photo courtesy of UIVC-P. Boillaud.

the sixteenth, seventeenth and eighteenth centuries, England was very keen on the 'black wine' of Cahors.

At the end of the nineteenth century, however, as in the rest of France, Cahors vineyards were wiped out by phylloxera. Stubborn and courageous, the winemakers replanted their vines, and, throughout the difficult times of the early twentieth century, they re-established their reputation. But their problems were not over. In February 1956 a big freeze settled over the entire country, wiping out olive, lemon and orange trees in Provence as well as all of Cahors' vineyards just to the North. Once more the stubborn winemakers replanted their vines. They used the strong Malbec grape for structure, sometimes mixed with Merlot or Tannat for more round and fruity flavors.

As a reward for their efforts towards quality and consistency, Cahors was granted AOC status in 1971 for its 4000 hectares of planted vines. Financially, however, little changed. Though well-perceived as a high quality wine, Cahors was losing ground in the international market. It needed a new marketing strategy.

In 2006, the professional association of Cahors winegrowers (Union Interprofessionnelle des vins de Cahors – UIVC) launched a new marketing campaign around two major concepts (Figure 4.2).

- Cahors is Back! Cahors is Black!
- Cahors is Malbec

The goal: to be different in order to be more effective in international markets, and to counter the competition of the red wines.

'Cahors is black' refers to the history of the wine. The Malbec grape growing on the Cahors *terroir* produces a very dark wine: Cahors is not red, it is dark. That is why, since the Middle Ages, it has been known as the 'black wine.'

But is black a trend in the wine business? To answer this question, on the initiative of their new Marketing Director, Jeremy Arnaud, the UIVC organized a convention there in February 2007 on the theme of the 'Black Paradox,' inviting to attend a college Professor, Michel Maffesoli, some wine professionals and a writer whose work studies colors and their meanings.

Figure 4.2   Poster of the Black Wine of Cahors
Source: Photo courtesy of UIVC-P. Boillaud.

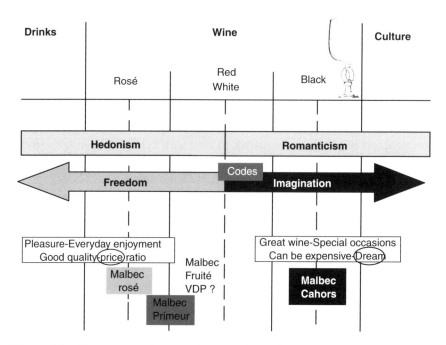

Figure 4.3   How young urban people rate wine colors

Source: Graph drawn from an original designed by UIVC, 2007.

What they found is that black appeals to young urban people. It relates to the world of luxury, imagination and culture in contrast to the three other wine colors shown above, in Figure 4.3.

Black also connotes the night, dreams, and mystery. When associated with wine it generates an emotional link with the product, which is often linked to younger consumers.

The second strong point of the Cahors wine is its grape, the Malbec. For many centuries in France it was called 'Auxerrois,' but the Cahors grape is, in fact, none other than the trendy Malbec. Malbec is one of the most sought-after grapes in Argentina and in many New World countries. It is popular in the United States and in the United Kingdom. Cahors has the privilege of being one of the most ancient and one of the best *terroirs* for Malbec. Marketing the wine as a variety wine with a special twist has great promise in the international market. Especially since, historically, the Argentinian winemakers cannot describe their wines as black.

Creating attention through a convention, and generating studies in French, does not carry any weight in the international market. That is why the UIVC created two blogs, blackisphere.fr and french-malbec.com, open to contributions from wine consumers, winegrowers and anybody else wishing to comment.

Thus far the result of the campaign has been fairly successful. The February 2007 convention drew the attention of many journalists and professionals and also resulted in an agreement among the winegrowers on the two major axes of the marketing strategy. Although figures for wine sales are not yet known, they are expected to show substantial increase.

Another oddity, the Müller-Thurgau grape

The Müller-Thurngau grape is famous in its country of origin, Germany, but is an oddity in the United States. It was created in late 1882 by Dr. Hermann Müller, who was born in the Swiss canton of Thurngau. At that time he was working in the German viticultural station of Geisenheim. His goal was to combine the quality of the Riesling grape with the reliability of the sylvaner.[1] Unfortunately, only a few producers were brave enough to try to market it alongside their more traditional Pinot Noir, Pinot Gris, Chardonnay and White Riesling grapes.

Although the type of wine made from the Müller-Thurgau grape is attractive to Americans, who are famous for their sweet tooth, the name – difficult to remember – and the fact that its variety was unknown were limiting its success. The dynamic Marketing Director of Château Benoit in Oregon, Peter Posert, was hired to turn the situation around. But what exactly was that situation?

- The variety was obscure, even to wine professionals.
- Consumers were not aware of the brand.

First, Peter directed his campaign at the professionals, thinking that, by educating the professionals, he would turn them into the best advocates of the wine. He organized a meeting of the 16 producers of the grape in Oregon. They decided on three actions:

- create a marketing brochure on the wine
- organize a seminar for the members of the Society of Wine Educators
- send their samples jointly to create awareness of the name.[2]

The first challenge for Peter and his colleagues was to collect enough information on the variety to convince professionals and consumers of the quality of the grape. Their big break came when it turned out that one of Oregon State University's professors had studied in Germany and Switzerland, and knew (almost) everything about the grape. The professor 'had a wealth of information and stories that made [their] research easy and professional.'[3]

The marketing brochure was then completed, and the dynamic team moved to organizing the seminar for the Society of Wine Educators. The seminar attracted over 50 specialists. From then on, the ball was set rolling. Samples of the wine were sent to magazines and journals with the brochure. The wines were rated in the eighties on a scale of 100, proving their quality.

The professionals were now aware of the wine. Consumers were the second main target. As articles were published in magazines, and wine reviews appeared, the consumers got interested enough to buy the wines.

Peter's team produced remarkable results in a short time: 'Prices started to rise and inventories started to shrink. After just three years of work, the planted acreage of Müller-Thurngau started to rise in Oregon again … Slowly the writers started to see something and the stories began. By the end of my time at Château Benoit, we were getting stories about every three months. The wine was featured on television, radio and many times in print around the country.'[4]

Segmenting or expanding the wine market

Capturing the millennial generation in the United States by segmenting the newcomers market

Market segmentation is a very important factor in the success of a strategy. It implies that wineries have a good knowledge of their customer base, and rely on professional studies. In the United States, the very recent phenomenon of the 'Millennials' attracted the attention of marketers and academics. Until the beginning of 2007 they were already aware of Generation X, supported by the famous *WineX* magazine, now defunct. However, 2007 saw the birth of the Millennials, those young people who reached the mature age of 21 after 2000 and are wine consumers. More precisely, a recent study showed alarming figures for the American wine industry. Millennials are more attracted to imports from countries like New Zealand, Chile, South Africa and Argentina than to American labels.

The figures reported in Table 4.1 for the Wine Market Council, a St. Helena trade group, in California, show the differences between the Millennials (age 21 to 30), Generation X (those from 31 to 42) and the Baby Boomers (those born in the years following World War II).

The Millennials are more imports-loyal for various reasons. First of all, they 'grew up with the assumption they could access just about anything at any price from anywhere and the only question was what suits their personal needs and choices as consumers,' said Wine Market Council President John Gillespie to journalist George Raine.[5] Then they are very open-minded towards any new consumable goods, and wine is part of this trend.

Capturing the millennial generation is critical to the wine industry. There are 76 million of them in the United States, compared to 44 million Generation Xers and 77 million Baby Boomers. How can the American wine industry attract those young people? First, the industry must inform them about American wines. California is the first area rising to the challenge. The California Association of Winegrape Growers launched in March 2007, a PR campaign informing professionals and consumers about the value of California wines.

Second, and maybe more to the point, some wineries have launched new brands specifically targeted at Millennials. Jess Jackson, founder of the Kendall-Jackson Winery, is one winemaker who has followed that course. In true American tradition, Jess Jackson buys his grapes all over California with careful selection to ensure quality and so improves the winemaking process to achieve seductive wines.

In July 2006, he launched a new company, the White Rocket Wine Company, whose President is Gary Glass, formerly Vice-President of

Table 4.1   Wine consumption differences by generation

	Domestic wines consumption	Imports consumption
Millennials	37%	32%
Generation X	57%	12%
Baby Boomers	67%	12%

Source: Created from data reported by George Raine.

Marketing for the Centerra division of Constellation Wines US. While there, Gary earned a reputation for creating some 'fun' labels, such as Monkey Bay and 3 Blind Moose. The new White Rocket Wine Company started with a foundation of brands including Camelot and Dog House. Tin Roof Cellars was later added to their portfolio as a result of the acquisition of Murphy Goode Winery by Jess Jackson.

White Rocket recognized that Millennials drink wine at a younger age than the Baby Boomers, and are ready to pay a higher price for their first bottle of wine. Why not take advantage of their tastes to offer them a very elegant and exclusive wine crafted for on-premises sale by the glass or in trendy restaurants? That is the idea behind Silver Palm Cabernet Sauvignon 2005, packaged in a beautifully designed bottle featuring a silver palm on a green bottle (see Figure 4.4). It was designed, says White Rocket Vice President of Marketing Mark Feinberg, 'to generate intrigue on-premise by instantly conveying superior quality, exceeding customer expectations and capturing the attention of diners at nearby tables.'[6]

This very special bottle and the on-premise sale strategy make the wine appealing to younger wine drinkers, who love the contemporary look and enjoy the quality of the wine.

In that context they have competition from the Rodney Strong Winery, owned by the Klein family.

Figure 4.4 Silver Palm Cabernet Sauvignon 2005 packaging

Source: White Rocket Wines Company.

Not wanting to dilute its image, Rodney Strong Winery created another company, Sonoma Vineyards, to target not only Millennials but also occasional drinkers or drinkers switching from beer to wine. This crossover of consumers benefits wineries with bold marketing policies: new labels with animals and funny names, 'fruity' easy-to-drink wines, screw-cap closures and descriptive back labels in layman's language. Based on such research, Sonoma Vineyards began its new line with a fruity 2003 Merlot wine and an 'unoaked' Chardonnay.

From Provence to the world: expanding from a local to a global market

The bold policies of a few American wineries should not overshadow the efforts of European wineries. Their own domestic markets, however, are usually too restricted in size making it necessary to expand out of their local markets. Thus the wineries always look to the highly desirable American scene, which requires a bold and courageous vision when targeting such a very competitive market.

One Provence winery did not hesitate to take the leap in a new project. Château Beaulieu (see Figure 4.5), a magnificent château located

Figure 4.5   Château Beaulieu
Source: Courtesy of PGA Domaines.

in the only volcanic crater in Provence, was bought in 2002 by the Guenant family, owners of an industrial empire. Beaulieu is located near the famed city of Aix-en-Provence in the heart of Provence, famous worldwide for sun, lavender, Cassis, St. Tropez, fragrances and aromas of flowers and herbs and the Mediterranean Sea.

Provence is also the birth place of dry rosé wine; 80 percent of the wines produced in this beautiful area are dry pink wines, the famed *Rosé de Provence*, the generic name of these wines. Their typical market is very local, since 80 percent of Rosés de Provence are sold in Provence itself to locals and tourists during the summer.

Why would a winemaker want to sell Rosés de Provence to British and American wine drinkers? In the United States, the blush wine market has fallen rather drastically in the last few years. Their very sweet taste and their poor-quality image are the two main reasons for taking consumers away from white Zinfandel and blush wines. At the same time, the market shows a small but continuous rise of interest in dry rosé wines. Provence producers want to take advantage of this trend to offer their own wines. The differentiating factor between Provence rosés and American pink wine is the quality and the more positive image of the wine in the American mind.

The UK market is different because there is a love-story between Provence and England. Many British people travel to Provence and the French Riviera several times a year, seeking sun and warmth. Many have even bought properties in Provence. Peter Mayle's book, *A Year in Provence*, and the recent movie, *A Good Year*, from his book popularized Provence in the British mind. Rosé de Provence is thus already known and recognized by the British as a quality wine.

Until recently, the French rosé wines available on the UK and the US markets were mostly those vinified by prestigious estates from Bandol or Tavel. There are also many American pink wines on the market, such as white Zinfandel, rosé from Merlot, Syrah or Cabernet grapes or the French-style rosé wines created by Jeff Morgan in his SoloRosa Winery in California.

How can these new markets be reached? To increase the visibility of its dry rosé wine and its attractiveness to the consumer, Château Beaulieu decided to simplify and clarify the product by creating one new generic brand called *Rosé de Provence* (Figure 4.6).

The two main characteristics of the wine are obvious from the label: it is a pink wine coming from the biggest producing area, Provence. Beaulieu is marketing a color (pink), a place (Provence) and a quality (dry).

Figure 4.6 Bottle of Rosé de Provence

Source: PGA Domaines.

The man behind the idea is James de Roany, General Manager of Château Beaulieu. Half British and half French and a former executive of the luxury brand Moët Hennessy, James has strong experience of both the Anglo-Saxon and international markets. He understood that to promote the area, Provence, and the wine, he needed to brand both together on a label and in a bottle, creating more value-added to expand visibility and build customer loyalty.

Launched in February 2007 on the French market, the wine hit the shelves with over 300,000 bottles. At the time of this writing, negotiations were on their way to access the British and the American markets, both of which are potentially interested in this concept.

As wine consumption in the US increases, consumers are becoming more interested in the winemaking process. A recent study shows that consumers are now inclined to learn more about wine history and the wine-making process rather than just learning how to taste. Some wineries are riding on this new trend, and use it to expand their visibility, as well as building more customer loyalty.

A special day at Château Palmer in Margaux, France

One of the rather obvious ways of attracting customers is to let the wine-drinking population share in the work of the winery. A few wineries all over the world welcome spe-cial guests or *aficionados* during the harvest. The guests are invited to work with the team for a few hours, share the lunch of the fieldworkers and end the day with a private tour and tailored tasting.

Château Palmer is one of the most beautiful and most distinctive wine estates in the famed Medoc region of Bordeaux. The château produces a wine sought-after throughout the world. In spite of its fame, the owners of Château Palmer enjoy welcoming guests and wine lovers. In 2001, under the direction of Bertrand Bouteiller, and using an idea of Bernard de Laage de Meux, the Development Director, Château Palmer intro-duced a special day for the members of their club called 'Experience the Harvest at Palmer.'

The agenda was quite appealing to the Palmer club members. At 8:30 a.m. sharp, Bertrand Bouteiller and Bernard de Laage wel-comed them and introduced them to the Palmer team. They were then assigned a plot of the vineyard where they were to pick grapes. The head of the team gave them careful instructions about the use of the secateurs, and how to select the ripest grapes. After three hours of back-breaking cutting, Palmer guests welcomed the lunch break they shared with the harvesters in the refectory of the château. In the afternoon they discovered the 'backstage' of the harvest: the arrival of the grapes, the sorting, the destalking and the grape crushing. They were allowed to share the vinification secrets and the mysteries of maturing in barrel, and to experience the magic of wine during a private tasting of older and young Palmer wines.

By opening its doors to their most faithful customers, Château Palmer increased their loyalty, and created a more emotional link with them. This tighter link with the end-consumer prompted the management to ask these privileged consumers to write about their passion. Canadian Daniel Paquette, who took part in a harvest in 2002, 'spent an unforgettable day picking grapes,' and since then has become a true Palmer *aficionado*: 'Opening a bottle of Palmer is always a celebration for me. It is the perfect accompaniment to game, and I have a special soft spot for Palmer and venison. In any event, I always bring out my best bottles for my closest friends.'[7]

From picking grapes to blending

But harvest happens only once a year for a few days. The rest of the year work goes on at the winery; crushing, fermenting, blending and bottling.

More and more wine consumers dream of making their own wines or at least a few bottles. That dream of consumers gave birth to the blending programs at various wineries in California. One of the pioneers is 'The Blending Cellar' in Glen Ellen, started by Jeff McEachern at the Mayo Glen Ellen Winery.

The idea was developed even further by the Bennett Lane Winery in Calistoga, California. The Bennett Lane Winery belongs to Randy and Lisa Lynch, who craft their red variety blend called *Maximus*, from Cabernet Sauvignon, Merlot and Syrah. Most of their wines are in the $30 range, which allows them to offer an up-scale experience to their customers.

Upon reservation, guests are invited to blend their own red wines in the Maximus style. This sophisticated program begins with a limousine service to and from the winery, allowing guests to enjoy themselves without worrying about naming a designated driver. Upon arrival, participants are guided to the barrel room where samples of the varieties are arranged on a table. The samples are taken from the French or American oak barrels where the wines are maturing. With the help of Stefanie Longdon, in charge of hospitality and marketing at the winery, they taste the samples, blend to their own taste, fill their bottle by hand with their own blend and label it. They are then taken to the tasting room for a private wine and cheese pairing session.

This personal and enjoyable experience lasts about three hours and costs $175 per person. It is an extremely good way to create an emotional link between the wines and the customer. 'We're all about people having an experience with the winery,' said Stefanie Longdon to journalist Tina Caputo, 'not just coming in and tasting, but learning where wine comes from and having their passion for wine start at our winery.'

Indeed, a better understanding of the wine-making process, as well as a personal connection with the winery staff and premises, leads to the reinforcement of the emotional link between customers and wineries. Wine drinkers love to be part of the harvesting and wine-making process – thus having the feeling that they own part of the wines they enjoy.

Communicating in an innovative way

In order to get noticed in the highly competitive world of wine, it is necessary to resort to very innovative techniques. Young winemakers – sometimes not from the trade and sometimes born on a vineyard – can be very imaginative, and open new roads to success and money.

SofiaMini, a young and trendy wine

Francis Ford Coppola is certainly one of the most famous American film directors of his time. Having directed *The Godfather*, *Apocalypse Now* and many other controversial movies that became classics within a few years, Francis Ford Coppola bought the Niebaum Winery in Rutherford, and named it the Niebaum-Coppola Estate Winery. In 1999, he launched a white sparkling wine, the Sofia Blanc de Blanc, named after his daughter. She was 28 at the time.

The success of this 'coup' has a great deal to do with the flamboyant personality of Sofia. At 19, she had already been awarded two Razzie awards for her lack of talent as an actress and her terrible temper – the Worst New Star and the Worst Supporting Actress. She soon realized that, instead of acting, she might be better off following in her father's footsteps and be a director. Her debut was in 1999 with *The Virgin Suicides* that won her a Young Hollywood Award for Best Director, and a MTV Movie Award for Best New Filmmaker. Her talent was confirmed with the romantic comedy *Lost in Translation* (2003) and her recent *Marie-Antoinette* (2006), a surprising but tender portrait of a young queen full of life and spirit, but trapped in a reactionary pre-revolutionary French royal court – *à la* Princess Diana.

The wine bearing her name is the very image of Sofia: 'revolutionary, poetic, ebullient, sparkling, energetic, fragrant, sweet, cool, petulant,' as the SofiaMini website declares.

What is Sofia Blanc de Blanc? It is a sparkling white wine packaged in a dark pink can and served with a straw. It is targeted at young urban women. The web site presents all the situations where you can drink this delightfully refreshing wine: while dressing to go out, while relaxing by the pool, talking on the phone to your friends, at a party, or taking your bath while your little cans cool in the bathroom sink. The SofiaMini is your everyday beverage sold in a four-can pack at the store. Just stop on the way to your dinner party to buy a pack and share it with your friends!

The message is clear. Wine is not just a serious business only for older wine geeks. It is fun, it is young, it is trendy, it is easy to drink (responsibly, warns the website). With its packaging and its ideas about consuming, SofiaMini is innovative and attractive to young drinkers like Sofia Coppola and her friends.

Young, fun, fresh, trendy all over the world

This message is becoming a kind of leitmotiv among winemakers, whether from the Old World or the New World. Wine is good, wine is easy to understand, wine is fun, wine is trendy. Following in the steps of Sofia Coppola, a few wineries designed fun and creative packaging for their wines. Barokes in Australia and French Lubie in Bordeaux are two examples.

Barokes wines claim they are the 'inventors of the innovative and patented wine in a can (Vinsafe™), a packaging system which enables premium quality wine to be canned with stability and longevity.'[8] Beginning in 1996, they have committed years of research to develop a range of wines for the global market.

The Australian Barokes wines come in various styles (varietal wines and blends) and even in four-can packs (see Figure 4.7). It is heavily marketed by the company. 'Today's global wine consumers are increasingly

Figure 4.7   Four-can pack of Barokes cans

Source: Courtesy of Akayama.

embracing simple means of beverage enjoyment, often in the new
economies where wine is seen as the modern trend from western culture.
Further than that, Generation X and Y drinkers from many diverse ethnic
origins are readily accepting ready-to-drink beverages of a spirit, wine
or soft drink base as the drink of the current era. Success in the beverage market comes from being chic, relevant, drink accessible, and
importantly single serve.'[9]

Barokes even trademarked the expression 'Ready to Drink Wines'
or RTDW to make sure they own the category! As they say in their
literature, it is great for camping, fishing, picnicking, and 'any
other outdoor activity.' The average consumer might just ask them one
single question: how do you drink your wine can when golfing or
bicycling? Maybe some common sense would have prevented such
silly advertising!

Apart from this little problem, the concept is very astute. The can is
protected by the Vinsafe technology 'which safely allows the sealing of
wine in a can to achieve premium quality, stability and longevity (up to
5 years to date).'[10] Their wines are now distributed all over the world and
on some airlines.

The French Lubie wine is a young Bordeaux-based company. In
strategy, as well as in its products, it is a little more subtle and elegant
than its American and Australian counterparts. Instead of aiming wildly
at a 'global' market, Lubie targets young and upper-scale consumers (see
Figure 4.8).

Figure 4.8 Lubie bottles
Source: Courtesy of Lubie.

Lubie was created in 2005 by two young women, Emmanuelle Blanc, who is an agricultural engineer, and her enologist friend, Marie-Laure Latorre. Four of their friends joined them in the adventure.

Emmanuelle and Marie-Laure based their product on two strong features: the innovative packaging and the high quality of their wines.

In 2005 and 2006, they targeted the young crowds in night clubs and the more mature wine drinkers in up-market wine and grocery stores in major cities.

Their primary target is female, since they describe the wine as 'feminine, natural, contemporary and self-indulgent' and believe women to be more sensitive to an elegant and unusual packaging. It is so much fun to show up for an evening with your pack of four small bottles of wine instead of a regular wine bottle! A young woman is featured as their symbol, both in their print material and on their web site (see Figure 4.9).

The Lubie concept is very close to the SofiaMini concept: the same targets (women and young consumers), the same style (easy to drink wines close to the soda world), the same innovative packaging and the same strategy.

Figure 4.9   Lubie – home page of the site (lubie.fr)
Source: Courtesy of Lubie.

What, then, makes it different from SofiaMini? Lubie presents two differentiating factors:

1. It is a variety wine, very easily identifiable by the consumer and of very high quality, since all come from an Appellation d'Origine Contrôlée (AOC or Controlled Appellation) area. Lubie comes in rosé (since Summer, 2007), Sauvignon blanc, Merlot and Cabernet Sauvignon, the three main Bordeaux grapes.
2. The packaging is light and environmentally safe, being biodegradable.

Lubie goes much further than SofiaMini: yes, wine is fun; yes, wine is easy to understand. But it is also a quality product, vinified by qualified winemakers and, as such, worthy of respect.

The Gallo family: an innovative repositioning strategy

The company E. & J. Gallo is the symbol of success in the American wine industry, reminding every wine drinker of its Californian pioneers, Ernesto and Julio. Julio died in 1993 in a car accident and Ernesto on March 7, 2007, 11 days before his 98th birthday. Joseph Gallo, the third brother, who was a cheese wizard and had been estranged from Ernesto for the previous ten years, died in February 2007. In that year, 2007, the first generation of the second biggest wine empire (Constellation Brands took the first place in 2003 after acquiring the Mondavi Empire) disappeared, leaving the grandchildren, Gina and Matt, in charge of the future. But this future started way back in 1975, when the first PR representative was hired. Let us go back in time!

The Gallo brothers 'founded E. & J. Gallo in 1933 in the Central Valley town of Modesto and grew the business into one that sells 75 million cases of wine a year, spread across 40 brands that are produced in five countries – the United States, Australia, Italy, France and New Zealand – and are exported to more than 80 countries.'[11] They started by making and selling very mediocre wines in the United States, as well as outside the country.

In the mid-1970s, Gallo launched new variety wines, foreseeing the switch of consumers from jug wines to more sophisticated ones. They hired a PR person, Dan Solomon, a veteran of the industry, to introduce the new wines into the domestic market. 'The first thing we did,' writes Dan, 'was hone and develop what I like to call the Gallo *quality story*.'[12]

By questioning the two brothers and their children, Dan found out that the Gallo winery had signed planting contracts with growers for quality grapes, and had a staff dedicated to counselling growers on growing a quality crop. On these basic facts, Dan developed a story validating the quality theme and created a press kit. E. & J. Gallo chose Charles M. Crawford, an enologist at the winery, as a spokesperson. Charles and Dan started meeting journalists and wine writers to present the new wines to them. They sent out samples, along with a personalized letter signed by Charles, entered contests and competitions, and won medals. They advertised their medals on shelf talkers and magazine ads.

Recognition came with the Gallo 1978 Cabernet Sauvignon, aged for 36 months in large oak barrels in Sonoma, and presented to the market in 1982. At that time, E. & J. Gallo had started buying and planting thousands of acres of grapes in Sonoma County. This new policy allowed them to create premium wines, and start the Gallo of Sonoma brand (now called Gallo Family Vineyards). Don invited people to visit the vineyards, and, instead of showing one more steel tank and another barrel, Dan organized the tour around the vines. Visitors left the property very pleased to have seen something different.

In 1995 Don left the Gallo winery after 20 years, and by that time the third generation of Gallos had stepped in. Gina and Matt Gallo were ready to talk to the press about their business, their hopes and their projects. They also talked of their love and respect for their parents and grandparents. Finally the public became aware of faces behind the names. Julio and Ernesto were presented as patriarchs as well as teachers of the young generation. 'You didn't grow up Gallo and not work,' Gina says to journalist Madelyn Miller from the *TravelLady Magazine*. 'The basic work ethic is very strong. By the time I was in grade school I was used to tagging along behind my older brother in the vineyard right by the house. He was pruning, which was his job, and my job was to help. I thought my job was to bug my brother. But we were both learning, both preparing, even when we were just hacking around in the vines.'

The family was photographed having a picnic or in the vineyard working. The values behind the image were explained: hard work, dedication and commitment. Gina was featured in magazine ads, and Matt spoke regularly to the press. Beautiful pictures of vineyards or family scenes appeared in glossy magazines and on TV.

The well-conceived PR move was to focus on the two younger members of the family, and mostly on Gina. Good-looking, nice, outspoken, driven, Gina is both the winemaker of the best Gallo vineyards in Sonoma and the spokesperson of the winery. Promoting Gina, who was promoting the best vineyards, made it a total success. It is not unusual to find a very positive and energetic portrait of Gina in the press, online and offline.

After the informal training of her youth, Gina studied business in college and signed up on the UC Davis wine-making program. She then went to work in the Gallo research winery, and got more and more interested in higher quality wines. Mentored by Marcello Monticello, one of the most respected Gallo winemakers, she was then promoted to the head of the Sonoma Vineyards, and is now advocating a very different wine-making style. 'Wine is pleasure,' Gina says to journalist Madelyn Miller. 'It has to be beautiful to look at, beautiful to smell, and astonishing to taste. I don't make obvious wines. I like depth. I like a little mystery, but I want some "wow!" in there somewhere, too. Wine should make you smile.'[13]

This very successful marketing strategy totally changed the image of E. & J. Gallo. The winery now has a very strong quality image associated with its name, mostly among young wine drinkers who never knew the days of the Gallo jugs.

Building a new business model: the wine clubs

When your name is not Gallo or Mondavi, with a large production sustained by big distributors, or when your name is not Margaux or Sassicaïa, with a small production but a very prestigious name, how do you sell your wines? The American industry came up with an innovative tool, the wine club. Wine clubs are a unique way of exploring a variety of wines with the convenience of regular door-to-door shipping.

Winery clubs: a good way to market wines

A club is part of a consumer direct-sales strategy, usually including a tasting room on the premises, some web sales and a mailing list.

How does a smaller winery club work? How is it managed? Who are its customers? Is it financially sound? Are wineries happy with the results of this strategy, or do they need improvement?

Whether they are operated by a winery to sell its own wines generally or by themes to target various types of customers, they are usually multi-leveled. There is the basic club shipping two bottles every month or two or every quarter and there is also the VIP club, called the 'Divine Club' at St. Supery, for example. Most small wineries have just a wine club without defining various levels. Subscription is free, but you have to buy a few pre-selected bottles. This situation raises some questions in the marketer's mind.

What are the pros and cons of a club for a smaller winery? First, the advantage is that it increases the margin by 30 percent to 40 percent by by-passing the distributor and the retailer. Second, smaller wineries might not even have access to big distributors, or might just be a line on a list of 5000 names. A good club will allow the smaller wineries to reach consumers directly, and to get some brand awareness. Last, but not least, a wine club is a very low-cost strategy.

The most frustrating disadvantage of a club is the shipment of the bottles. In the United States, the legacy of Prohibition, as we noted earlier, is a very complex distribution system, called the three-tier system. Tier one is represented by the producers and suppliers, tier two by the distributors, wholesalers and brokers and tier three by the retailers (wine stores, restaurants, hotels, cruises, wine bars and so on). The wine is then available to the consumer, sometimes called the fourth tier! A producer from California can ship only to some states – frustrating for the others: Alaska, Florida, Idaho, New York, Texas (some restrictions for these states); California, Colorado, Connecticut, Illinois, Louisiana, Massachusetts, Missouri, Nebraska, Nevada, New Hampshire, New Jersey, New Mexico, North Carolina, North Dakota, Ohio, Oregon, Virginia, Washington, Washington D.C., West Virginia, Wyoming (no restrictions).

The situation is little better in Europe, despite the free trade zone called the 'Schengen space,' which includes the euro countries, where merchandise can be shipped and received without any taxes. The wine and food business is more regulated at the national level than other economic sectors. In Austria, for example, the winery must have a legal representative to import its wines. The Scandinavian countries have a State monopoly on wine imports, and are only gradually opening to free trade. These rules of course inhibit the winery from generating a profitable business.

Does a wine club help a winery know its top consumers? All wineries collect names, addresses and email addresses, and reinforce the links by sending newsletters, invitations to special events and sometimes an email. Most of the small wineries know their 50 top consumers. They are the people coming to wine events, visiting the winery regularly and buying a lot of cases. Bigger wineries have more sophisticated ways of building customer loyalty: consistent quality, low prices, strong distribution strategy and discounted prices play their part.

Is the wine club the most effective marketing tool for a small winery? Wine clubs come only second after the tasting room. The tasting room indeed accounts for at least 51 percent of direct sales. The wine club brings from 11 percent to 50 percent of the direct sales. Sales through returns from the mailing list account for a modest 2 percent.

To enjoy Californian wines join the California Wine Club!

There are clubs geared for a variety of wine enthusiasts: Red Wine Clubs, International Wine Clubs, White Wine Clubs, winery wine clubs, sweet and dessert wine clubs, regional Wine Clubs, and the list goes on and on.

What are the advantages for both parties? On the customer side, there is no shopping, no delivery problem, full refund guarantee in case of corked or damaged bottles, access to wines difficult to find or not available on the shelf, no distributor, no middleman and the best choice of wines at the lowest possible price, savings on normal retail price and very often a beautiful catalog full of fun information and tips. Extra bonus: 'the research and work have been done for the consumer,' explains Gerri-Lynn Becker, Marketing Director of the California Wine Club. 'The task of selecting a good wine is daunting and confusing. With the right wine club, the member can be guaranteed of quality, great taste and convenience. And may even be introduced to a wine or a winery that's little known.'

On the winery side, being selected by a good club, like the California Wine Club, is a major asset. 'We only feature wines from small, real working wineries,' explains Gerri-Lynn. 'Most of the wineries we feature don't produce enough to reach mass distribution. There is a real-live family behind each wine and we introduce their story and passion to our members.' This brings a totally different dimension to the relationship between the Club, the winery and the member, creating an emotional link between them and benefitting the club as the provider of a very enjoyable experience. 'We bring the romance of wine country to the members,' confirms Gerri-Lynn. 'By getting to know the who/what/ where of each wine, it makes the experience more personal and the wine even better.'

Wine clubs like the California Wine Club are highly popular in the United States and have a wide range of customers – from neophytes to connoisseurs. For Gerri-Lynn, 'they all seem to have something in common: they like the adventure of trying something new and trust us.' Their behavioral patterns are subject to change but they are still 'typical of the industry. For example, ten years ago no one was drinking Bordeaux blends … yet now they're quite popular! And this past year we're seeing a big push towards Rhone-style wines. Also we've noticed over the years that more customers are sending gifts of wine. Even corporate gift givers are breaking away from fruit and chocolate and looking to send something more unique and exciting.'[14]

'In vino caritas': compassion marketing

Thanks to Don and Petie Kladstrup, we now have a new segment in wine marketing – *compassion marketing* (known to marketers as 'social marketing,' of course) as they developed it in their article, 'In Vino Caritas: Drinking Well and Doing Good,' published in *The World of Fine Wines* (Issue 17, 2007). If some ill-fitted initiatives, like the pink-ribbon one for breast cancer of Sutter Home can backfire, a well-thought-out and valid cause can gain support from the wine community as well as from the consumers. Why is it that wine is a good support for charity? 'Much of it has to do with the magic and prestige wine brings to any fundraising event,' explain the Kladstrups. Animals and environmental issues are very often embraced by wineries, but the medical and social fields are more rewarding for the winemakers or the owners.

Two French winemakers, Michel Chapoutier, from the Rhone Valley, and Michel Rolland, from Château Le Bon Pasteur in Bordeaux, joined forces to raise awareness on bone-marrow transplants and the urgent need to find more donors to save lives.[15] The story began in 1994 when Michel Chapoutier saw the photo of a little girl in need of a bone-marrow transplant: 'As a father, I felt I had to do something,' Chapoutier said. He issued a call for help. 'If you'll help me pick grapes free for one day, I'll donate your wages plus some of my own money to help fund bone-marrow transplants.' More than 100 people showed up to pick grapes in September 1994, but, after the death of the little girl, Chapoutier decided to go even further. During a conversation with his friend, wine consultant and winemaker Michel Rolland, about eighteenth- and nineteenth-century wines and how Hermitage was so expensive, an idea came to them. In those days, some Hermitage wine was added to Bordeaux wines to make the latter stronger. The two Michels decided to give a second life to this style of wine, a 'Bordeaux hermitagé,' which they called M2. The first vintage was born in October 2007, and will be sold online in November for the benefit of a foundation Chapoutier has created, to fund bone-marrow transplants and research into blood diseases.

When Don and Petie asked what compelled Chapoutier to launch this initiative and create a foundation, he answered: 'When I bought my vine-yard from my grandfather, it was in bankruptcy. When you do something like that, you can become obsessed with money and making it profitable. You can loose your soul that way. I felt I needed to do something to keep my soul in good health.' Then he laughed and said. 'I suppose you could say that in one way this is a very selfish project.'

What happens to traditional tools?

Through these few examples of basic marketing strategies used in the New and the Old World, we have made a brief but incomplete survey of the major marketing tools available to wineries and wine estates in general. What is the common denominator of those strategies? They are the traditional centralized models of creating and distributing informa-tion. The receivers are supposed to believe and accept what marketers and producers are saying, writing and publishing. This is the 'top-down message strategy' used since Day 1 of advertising.

Are these tools now meaningless and useless for our new consumers? Maybe not. They are still the way a lot of traditional and older consumers relate to a brand or a product or to news about them. They are also the basic tools used to develop new technological tools. After all, a press release, a brochure or a newsletter is liable to disappear, but, on the Web, they will circulate and have a life of their own through web communities, blogs, forums, podcasts, RSS threads, Google and Yahoo! News and alerts. They will be scrutinized, analyzed and sometimes rejected by the consumers, and they will be subjected to a lot of questioning. But they will still be there.

Bottom line? Winemakers and producers, distributors and participants in the wine industry have to learn how to master the web marketing tools, and, more importantly, learn how to communicate directly with their customers.

CHAPTER 5

Pouring wines in new ways: marketing on the Web 1.0

In the old days – prehistoric times for the Web – about 1995, an American woman, living in France and owner of one of the most prestigious Bordeaux estates, was painfully surfing the Net on a Compuserve connection at 9600 bps. She read people's comments on her wines, and their version of the history of her beautiful Château. She thought it would be better to be in control herself of information about her company, as well as its image. In this way she could provide valuable and reliable information about making the wines, and the history of the estate and of Bordeaux, as well as providing tasting notes. That is why, and how, the first web site of one of the five Classified First Growths of Bordeaux, Château Haut-Brion, was born in 1996. Then the four others, at first very skeptical, built their own web sites in the following years.

Because of the foresight of its President, Joan Dillon, Duchess of Mouchy, Domaine Clarence Dillon, which owns Château Haut-Brion, the oldest and the smallest of the five, now has the oldest and the biggest web site. The construction of the web site was very carefully thought out and planned under the Duchess' supervision. First, a small web site was created around Château Haut-Brion. A few months later, each of the other estates owned by Domaine Clarence Dillon had a dedicated web site: Château La Mission Haut-Brion, Château La Tour Haut-Brion, Château Laville Haut-Brion, Bahans Haut-Brion and Les Plantiers. Over the years, Domaine Clarence Dillon added features to the web site on wine-making technologies, videos on decanting and the history of the estates, flash technology and blog technology. First available in French and English, the site was later translated in German, Spanish, Japanese and Simplified as well as Mandarin Chinese. The site now includes hundreds pages of information in each language. The Château develops a new design every three years to keep the site technically up-to-date and graphically elegant.

The first online tool: the web site

Web sites were the first tools available for marketing on the Web. The hyperlink technology, the accessibility from anywhere in the world for anyone having an Internet connection and a computer, seemed a wonder to many. Just saying your company had a web site put you in a very special category in the early years of the Internet, especially in Europe. Unfortunately for the wineries, web surfers very soon became technically more savvy, and having a web site was no longer enough to make a difference. The web site had to be efficient and answer to the needs of the customers. Those were the days when web marketers began telling their clients: 'Don't create a web site for yourself; create it for your customers! Ask yourself what you would like to find on your web site if it was the first time you had come across it!' How did this translate in the wine business? The best sites address the needs of four types of visitors: buyers, Internet users, the trade and the media. An effective site must help visitors accomplish what they came to do without a lot of wasted effort. A web surfer is a potential customer. Trade is the best link to potential customers, and the press can be the free PR a winery, small or big, needs so much!

The first-generation web sites were very simple technically, and also very simple in their goals: to put in front of the world the history of the estate, the qualities of the wines and some basic information. Within two years, email became more important and was soon a major communication tool, often replacing the phone and the fax. Fast connections were developing and becoming more available to private homes as well as businesses. The fast connections, whether DSL or cable, made software companies work on more user-friendly software to build web sites. It was the golden times of: 'Be on the Net for $20! Build your own web site yourself!' Software became more sophisticated by the late 1990s with Flash technology; designers became stars and sites almost works of art.

A golden picture? Not at all. One important group of characters was totally absent from this rosy picture: the Internet users, the potential customers. Let us call them Ben and Linda, Pierre or Martine, Chandra, Li or Natasha. Fighting with Flash sites on low speed connections, Ben and Linda had to be online for hours, at their own expense, looking for the information they were entitled to get. Frustrated consumers were getting mad at the Internet world. The companies on the Net were wondering why they did not get a satisfactory return as a result of their investment. After all, building a web site was very costly.

How could the two worlds get back together? Web marketing went into action. Marketers from the traditional world were at a loss with this new technology, but help came from the academic and publishing world. Professionals already used to analyzing and synthesizing information from various backgrounds and sources started formalizing the problems and inventing new solutions. Another problem appeared – each country was different. Strangely enough, the United States stayed on low speed connection much longer than Europe and Japan. Japan was very much ahead of all the other countries. It had high speed connections, Flash technology and 3G mobiles before anybody else. In Europe, Italy was leading for three years before losing ground and allowing France, England and Germany to take the lead. This very simple technical consideration meant that the rate at which people became connected grow at different speeds! Consequently, the number of people connected varied greatly from one country to another (Table 5.1):

Table 5.1   Country Internet connection by year

Country	2006	2005	2002	1999
USA	63.6%	60.6%	72%	59%
China	10.2%	7.2%	–	–
Japan	68.4%	57.2%	47%	33%
UK	57.9%	53.4%	50%	33%
India	2.3%	2.0%	–	–
France	47.1%	–	37%	22%

Source: Journal du Net, 2007.

Japan, the United Kingdom and the United States are now the three leading countries in numbers of connected people. The United States lost their first place to Japan. India and China are now joining the club, and growing slowly but steadily.

Re-inventing old tools

Marketers understood that web sites could not be the only marketing strategy on the web. They examined the old tools – newsletters, mailings, and so on – and adapted them to the new technology. The only problem was the accuracy of a mailing list. No company could sell mailing lists with accurate email addresses. Wineries had to rely on their existing paper mailing lists, and ask their customers for their email addresses. Some did not have one yet, or refused to give it. That is why some companies started offering free information or goodies to get the email addresses of potential customers. It was a win-win situation for both parties.

One of the first Bordeaux estates to apply this strategy was Château Palmer, a classified growth in Margaux. Château Palmer is owned by three families, the British Sichel family, the Dutch Mahler-Besse family and the French Bouteiller family. Château Palmer came rather late to the Web: their first site was launched in 2001, when most of the estates in the Bordeaux area were already working on their second or even third versions. Like a lot of Bordeaux estates, Palmer sells its wines through the Bordeaux marketplace run by the *negociants* or wine brokers. Because of this situation, the managers find access to the retail level difficult, and do not really know who the end-consumers are, except for a few collectors of international fame.

The web site became the core of their PR and communication strategy. Because the site was created when the technology and the marketing strategies were already well implanted, the managers very cleverly used the experience of the other estates and web marketers to keep ahead of the competition. They envisaged a site in four parts: one for the wine drinkers, one for the sommeliers, one for the trade and another for the press. Each of those sections had a slightly different content to answer the specific needs of each category, and each category had a specific color. This very contemporary approach, as well as a colored and elegant design, made the Palmer site stand out.

But the truly new marketing tool was the 'Club' idea. In order to access the full content of the site, as well as to gain some special privileges, consumers, trade, sommeliers and media had to register, and become a member of the club. Given the prestigious name of the Château, registrations were – not surprisingly – high in each category.

The idea was to generate customer loyalty by allowing a few club members to spend a day in the vineyards during harvest time. In the morning club members joined the team of harvesters and cut grapes. Although most of them thought it was a 'back-breaking job,' they thoroughly enjoyed it. 'The idea of being part of the making of a vintage of Chateau Palmer is exhilarating,' said a happy and tired participant. After work, the reward: the participants shared the harvesters' meal in the big dining-room of the Château. In spite of the noisy background created by the conversation of almost 100 young people and the restorative food, participants enjoyed eating at the table of the management, and asking any questions they wished. After lunch came a private tour of the estate, and a tasting of an older Château Palmer vintage, followed by a barrel tasting of the vintage ageing in the *chais* next door. What an exceptional experience!

This strategy paid off. Some participants asked to come back the next year. Word spread on the Internet, and some club members published the newsletter privately and advertised the initiative of the Château on their own. This buzz-marketing generated more subscriptions to the club.

In order to thank those faithful and well-disposed customers the Château developed another initiative: inviting the club members to the 'Oeufs Moreau' party. What are the 'Moreau Eggs'? Moreau is the name of a couple, M. and Mme. Moreau, who worked at the Château for many years. To fine the wine, usually in January and February, the Château uses about 5000 egg-whites. That means the Château is left with about 5000 egg yolks. Traditionally, the yolks were sold to nearby bakeries for their pastries, but one year, at the end of the fining season, the Moreau couple suggested organizing a party with all the employees and the management to celebrate the occasion. The yolks available that day are put on grills over a fire of dead vines just cut from the vineyard. The Palmer team gathers around the fire where the eggs cook, and share them. Out of consideration for the cholesterol level of the team, the 'Moreau Eggs' party only happens once a year!

Like the Harvesting Day Experience, the Moreau Eggs Party has enjoyed great success. Many club members come to the Château in the middle of winter to celebrate the end of a very important process in the *chais* with the Palmer team.

The Château Palmer strategy was multi-leveled, but originated in a very clever use of parts of its web site. Privatizing access to its web site was innovative in 2001, when the general policy was to access the world through a web site. Palmer instead opted for an exclusive strategy, positioning itself as marketing not merely a product, but a luxury product. This positioning is not a particularly common strategy among wineries, but it had very positive results. It obtained better knowledge of its end-consumers, better contacts with the trade and the restaurants through their sommeliers and a privileged relationship with the online press, which was developing at that time.

Inventing new tools

Other wineries in Bordeaux came up with new tactics to get a better knowl-edge of their end-consumers, and to develop a relationship with them. The forum is one of the best strategies used by wineries and by the press.

A very useful innovation: the forum

As soon as their first site was launched in 1996, Château Haut-Brion created a forum linked to the site (Figure 5.1). The purpose was to encourage the end-customers to ask the Château their questions instead of looking for information on the Net. The President of the company, Joan Dillon de Mouchy, was convinced that good and reliable informa-tion had to be provided by the company, so that it could be spread over the Net. It was a brilliant tactical move, and, after 12 years on the Web, most information circulating on the Web about the various estates belong-ing to Domaine Clarence Dillon is based on the web site.

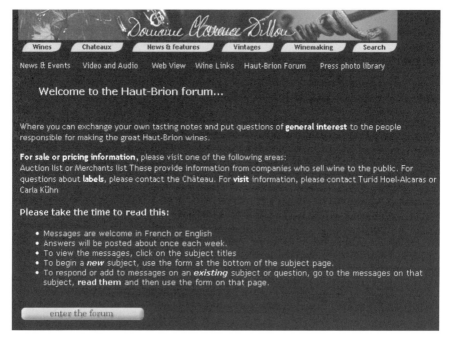

Figure 5.1   Homepage of the Haut-Brion forum

Source: Courtesy of Domaine Clarence Dillon.

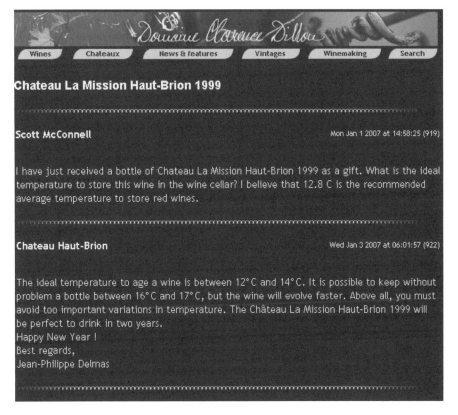

Figure 5.2   A page from the Haut-Brion forum

Source: Courtesy of Domaine Clarence Dillon.

The forum that is run on the web site addresses any questions relating to the wines of Domaine Clarence Dillon, wine and food pairing, or the drinkability of a bottle (Figure 5.2). One of the managers is mandated to reply quickly to the questions.

Forums are an extremely effective tool to interact with end-customers, and create, or reinforce, an emotional link with them. They encourage the end-customers to have conversations between themselves, to share their impressions and their feelings, benefitting from the guidance and supervision of the Château.

In 2006, the Haut-Brion forum addressed 44 topics within a wide range of subjects: among them an extensive discussion on the 1974 vintage, monitored by manager Jean-Philippe Delmas, another one on the 1964 Haut-Brion, questions and discussions about pairing food with specific vintages and many others.

An analysis of the forum topics showed a strong interest in the vintages and their drinkability, as well as good food pairing. This trend is confirmed by the stream of visitors to the Vintages and tasting notes pages on the Haut-Brion site.

Online wine magazines and forums: journalists on the Net

Winery forums do have their limitations for end-consumers and wine lovers. First of all, most subjects are about the wines of that estate, and are closely monitored by the management. That leaves no space for exchanges on wine and food in general. Journalists answered this new need of the consumer by creating their own magazines online, and linking them to a discussion forum, where wine buffs and food *aficionados* could exchange ideas and tips, as well as debate the multiple issues of the wine world, such as the importance of '*terroir*,' the qualities of the various vintages, the grapes and many other fascinating topics.

The British journalist Tom Cannavan has been writing about wine and food since the early 1990s. He was also an Internet pioneer, launching his wine-pages.com online magazine in 1995. He also writes extensively in print. He was editor of *Fine Expressions* from 2005 to 2006 and currently has regular columns in two magazines, contributing to *Wine report* and the *Which?* Annual wine guides. His work has appeared under many titles, including *Decanter*, *Wine & Spirit*, *The World of Fine Wines* and *Harper's* magazines. Tom is also in demand as a wine judge, and has been a panelist at competitions in Australia, Argentina, Chile, France, the United Kingdom and Georgia.

I was in contact by email with Tom for many years before actually meeting him in Paris. Tom is passionate about wine and food and has traveled extensively around the world, tasting wine and food. He has a fine knowledge of restaurants all over the world and I felt a little nervous when he suggested I make a reservation in a restaurant I enjoyed – even in my home city, Paris. I still do not know if I made the right choice because, being extremely gracious, Tom approved of my choice (or at least did not complain).

When Tom started his virtual adventure with wine-pages.com (see homepage in Figure 5.3 on next page) in 1995, he saw the Internet 'as a fantastic new means of communication, with its ability to spread and share high quality information at low-cost, and with no geographical boundaries.' To him, the Internet was 'a wonderful and liberating media, with low costs, editorial freedom and instant access

Figure 5.3   Homepage of wine-pages.com site
Source: Courtesy of Tom Canavan.

to one's readership.' For instance, he can post his notes on the Bordeaux 'En Primeurs' (Futures) season instantly on his site, giving his readers the very latest information at this crucial time for the Bordeaux economy. In spite of providing information so rapidly, he keeps a very high standard of writing and tight editing. 'Also,' says Tom, 'it is great that everything I have ever written for the web site – 12 years of writing, six days per week, is still accessible, which builds wine-pages and sites like it into wonderfully rich and deep resources that print media can't easily manage.'[1]

At first, he was not aware of the commercial possibilities of the new media. In 1999, he started selling advertising on his site: by 2007, he had 'a broad portfolio of wine businesses as clients,' many of whom have worked with him for six years or more. 'I have proved – both to myself and my clients – that the Internet is amongst the most effective forms of advertising media available today,' says Tom.

Going further in the development of his web site, Tom created a forum open to wine lovers and professionals. How did he manage to create a large and lively online community? Interactivity was a key part of the site from the beginning with discussion forums, quizzes, polls, community-built resources like tastings and events diaries, but also regular features such as the Readers' Wines of the Year. The forum is now very active with more than 300 people logged on at any one time of the day or night. The participants post tasting notes, share valuable information on wine, vintners, restaurants, wineries, wine and food pairings, and the like. Over the years, this community has developed strong ties, and some members meet occasionally for dinners referred to as *offlines*.

Through his web site and forum, Tom Cannavan contributed to the building of an international community of wine drinkers and consumers. By 2004 Tom realized his site attracted almost 400,000 visitors per month, 'making it one of the world's most influential wine titles in any media,' as he found out with pride. Why not extend this success to the beer and whisky lovers so numerous in the United Kingdom? In 2005, Tom added beer-pages.com to his publishing stable, employing Roger Protz as editor, and in 2006 whisky-pages.com became his third title, edited by Gavin D. Smith. Both sites 'are doing very well,' reports Tom with pleasure, 'using the same blend of news, reviews and high quality features, plus interactive elements like polls, forums and competitions.'

Email marketing

Mailing – and its online extension, e-mailing – is a strategy in full development. In Europe 75 percent of the companies use email campaigns. Their reasons are different.

Table 5.2 shows very clearly that emailing is used mostly for promoting or providing information on products, and to encourage the recipients to buy and generate more sales. Collecting information on the

Table 5.2   Reasons for using email marketing (percent)

Build the image of the brand	38%
Make the brand the favorite of the consumers	66%
Collect information on the consumers	77%
Increase sales	90%
Generate more buys	93%
Information on products, services, news	97%

customers comes fourth when collecting any data regarding branding is not the primary target of the companies.

Online magazines and emailing

To keep his community's interest alive, Tom Cannavan sends a personalized monthly newsletter featuring the latest news on his wine web site.

The email's recipient is reminded of the magazine and sent to the site by links to the main sections (Figure 5.4 below).

Dear Evelyne,

Welcome to wine-pages.com's October newsletter.

There is a whole heap of wine merchants offering wine-pages readers the chance to win prizes, or receive some really good discounts on wine purchases. Wine-pages makes absolutely nothing on these deals – no referall fees, commissions or kick-backs – but with 25 companies now advertising on wine-pages.com, several have made genuine discounts available to encourage the site's readers to try their services – no strings attached.

Figure 5.4   Emailing from wine-pages.com

Source: Courtesy of Tom Canavan.

Wineries and emailing strategies

In continental Europe, wineries send emailings mostly to build the image of their brand. This strategy will apply mostly to the Classified Growths in Bordeaux and very prestigious estates. The more modest winery will send an email in order simply to sell its wines.

Château Palmer was one of the first Classified Growths of Bordeaux to launch a Newsletter, as early as 2001, and called it 'Palmer Letter', shown in the design of the old site (Figure 5.5) and in the current design (Figure 5.6) on next page. It was available in English, French and German, and had a different content for each group it was addressed to – the Club members, the press or the trade. The newsletter was branded by use of color on the site.

The newsletter's purpose is to inform the club members of the events taking place at the estate. It is very personalized, and is signed by the Marketing Director as if written by hand.

Figure 5.5   A Club Palmer mailing on the old site (2001–04)

Source: Château Palmer.

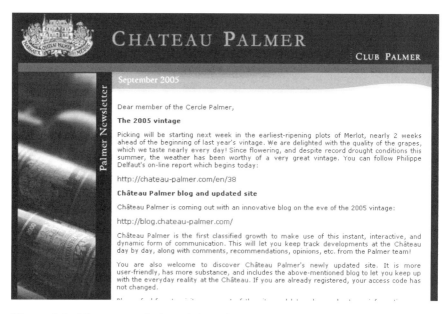

Figure 5.6   The current design of the Palmer Letter

Source: Château Palmer.

The newsletters of lesser estates wanting to sell their wines or advertise their latest releases are very different. The Château Ducru-Beaucaillou in the Saint-Julien appellation in Bordeaux advertised the release of its new vintage in a well designed newsletter (Figure 5.7).

Unfortunately, the newsletter is totally impersonal and cold. It is signed 'Château Ducru-Beaucaillou,' and carries just a quotation from Bruno Borie. Is he the owner? If you do not know who is who and who does what, you will not know much more after reading this newsletter. This email does not entice the recipient to click on the clever link to learn more. But does our consumer Ben really care? The purpose of the newsletter is to sell him the 'futures' from the estate, and Ben may very well not be interested. The mailing will go into the bin.

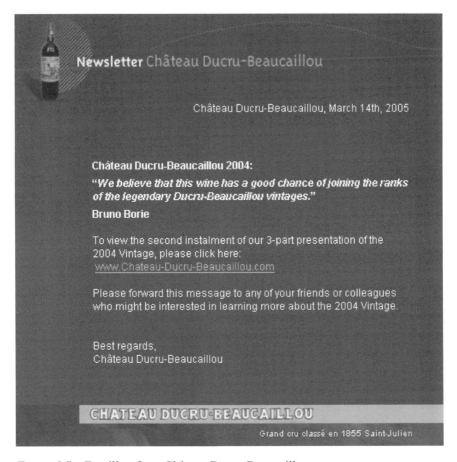

Figure 5.7   Emailing from Château Ducru-Beaucaillou

An emailing strategy has to be well thought-out before being sent. Because the cost of an email is not very high, a lot of wineries think they can send them as often as they wish. This policy does not take into account the amount of emails Ben and Linda in the United States, Pierre and Marie in France, Li in China, Natasha in Russia or Chandra in India receive every day. Bothered by too many meaningless mailings, they will send the message to the trash bin without even looking at it. The next message will generate a cancellation of subscription, or, even worse, a spam report.

What is the right strategy for emailing? When Ben, Linda, Li, Chandra, Pierre or Natasha subscribe to a newsletter, the sender must thank them, and add some informative text. If he/she wisely asks them, and obtains, their birthday or the birthday of their sweetheart, why not send them a little note suggesting a gift or a good bottle for celebration? In other words personalize your relationship with them as much as possible. This is the secret of success, creating an emotional link between your wine and your customers or trade partners.

What is the return on investment in such campaigns? When no commercial profit is sought or needed, the return is a better image of your brand and a better connection with your customer. When you do want to sell something, look carefully at the financial return and orders.

Emailing in retail businesses

In the United States, the emailing strategy is widely used by wine clubs, wineries and retail stores as well as wine and/or lifestyle magazines. The return on investment through their mailings is crucial to their business.

In Charlotte, North Carolina, Henry and Barbara Tyree realized their life's dream in 2006, opening a wine store and wine bar, *Under The Grape*, in the newly constructed high-class Ballantyne Village. It was not an easy task. Henry was a college professor and Barbara was a USAir flight attendant. Their passion is wine, and, in their spare time, Barbara and Henry scouted Charlotte for the wines they loved, and a nice place to enjoy them. Guess what? They had a hard time finding their wines, and the cool place to enjoy them did not exist in lovely Charlotte. That is how the idea of *Under The Grape* was born, a beautiful wine store with a very elegant wine bar on top. The Tyree's first step was to get credentials. Both went back to school for the certifications required to open a wine business. Fortunately, the courses at the Society of Wine Educators allowed them to keep working at their day jobs and to study at night, while, at the same time, working on their business plan. After three years of hard work and a great deal of emotional stress, *Under The Grape* opened its doors on a gorgeous day in May 2006. The wine store and the elegant wine bar, with its delightful patio, provide a place for customers to enjoy a glass of cool wine while snacking on delicate dishes. Word of mouth and curiosity about the new shopping center attracted a good crowd during the spring and the summer. Barbara immediately started collecting email addresses on a list placed next to the cash register. Almost every customer or passer-by registered, and more inquiries by emails came in through the web site.

Barbara and Henry put the mailing list to its best use. Every week, they would send the agenda of their tastings and the music program of the bar (Figure 5.8). Matter-of-fact, but always nicely written and with a zest of humor, the emailings drew clients to the store and the bar, as well as spreading the buzz. After all, as the Tyrees realized, forwarding an email to a friend is just a click away.

After a year and a half of business, Barbara Tyree thinks the emailing was 'our most powerful marketing tool.' Customers keep coming back for tastings, classes, a glass at the bar with friends and to take home a few bottles.

Figure 5.8 Example of an emailing by Under the Grape
Source: Courtesy of Under the Grape.

Press online and offline: duet or duel by email?

The online and the offline press very soon realized the efficiency of emailing for sustaining their magazines. This strategy is also used by print media that has gone virtual over the years. Most of the print media now have a web site, with contents which are different from the print version, but also linked to it. Examples are *Decanter* and *The World of Fine Wines* in the United Kingdom, and *The Wine and Food Magazine* in the United States, for instance.

As early as 1996 in the United States, wine and lifestyle magazines were on the Net. At first they just published a developed table of the contents of their print magazine. Then they understood they had to provide better and more appropriate content to the web surfer. Indeed, the Internet user very often bought the monthly magazine, but also wanted to receive information faster. The magazines opened sections giving facts or news on their web site in order to answer that need, modeled on 'breaking news' on television.

The *Food and Wine Magazine* web site provides 'Web Exclusives,' giving 'speedy weeknight recipes' with their wine pairings, interviews and exclusive recipes, among other features. It also offers a searchable database of all the restaurants they have mentioned in their print issues. Last, but not least, the magazine created a Connoisseur Club, allowing its members 'to get exclusive savings on merchandise, cookware, specialty foods, wine and more.' The Connoisseur Club has its own site, theconnoisseurclub.com, featuring all its advantages: a specialty shop, culinary travel organized through partnerships with travel agencies and cruises, special offers in the 'dining out' section in some of the major cities of the United States, wine classes and discounts on wines, and significant savings on Wine and Food events. For the club membership of $149 a year, you also receive:

- Exclusive discounts on specialty food, rare wines, quality cookware, and other offers from the Club's Preferred Partners.
- Discounted admission to and extra amenities at the world's best food and wine events.
- Savings on travel from the top epicurean tour and cruise companies.
- Convenient online dining reservations with their partner OpenTable.com.
- Quarterly newsletter and Partner Mailings containing special savings opportunities.[2]

Bon Appetit and *Gourmet Magazine* joined forces to launch the site epicurious.com 'for people who love to eat.' In addition to recipes, special features on food, wine, traveling, *Gourmet* and *Bon Appetit* offer both 'Web exclusives' featuring recipes, special offers and newsletter subscriptions. *Wine&Spirits* magazine offers a 'subscribers only' section featuring a wine search, a shopper's guide and a restaurant poll. The added-value of this section is tremendous.

Most of the web sites of those magazines have in common their wish to convince the web surfer to subscribe to the print version. They provide

Figure 5.9   Example of an emailing from decanter.com on the next print issue

Figure 5.10   Example of a daily News Alert from decanter.com

News | Recommendations | Wine Finder | Decanter World Wine Awards | Events | Learning Route | Fine Wine Tracker

Welcome to decanter*trade*

You lucky people. Apparently our 'sommelier speaks' section of decanter*trade* is a bit of a hit, so this time we're featuring an extended interview wit h **Damien Trinckquel** at Sheen Falls Lodge in Ireland. Of course, if you want the most interesting bit, you'll have to wait for the December issue of Decanter magazine (out 5 Nov - which is also the day of the **Pomerol trade tasting** - see below for details). The issue also features our **Wines of the year** - don't miss it.

Other news, and we've got a lot of panel tastings coming up: **Crus Bourgeois** and **St-Emilion '05** have been added to the list. Bloc Cellier are looking for a representative in the UK, and as ever, we've got jobs, news and events to tell you about.

For those of you that are wondering how we found out you like the sommelier speaks section - you told us on the **decanter.com survey**. Thanks to all of you who took part.

Trade news
from decanter.com

- Petrus successor named as Moueix appoints new director
- Boomerang takes flight in the US
- Peru's wine regions continue to feel aftermath of earthquake
- Unauthorised Parker biography ignites passions
- Record harvest in Champagne
- Pinot Noir overtakes Cabernet in Sonoma County, Merlot is 'dismal'

Figure 5.11 Example of an emailing from decantertrade

just enough content to attract but frustrate the reader, and send him to the subscription section. This aim is clearly stated in the emailings sent to their opt-in subscribers, such as the one shown in Figure 5.9 from decanter.com in their November 2007 issue.

To complement its print edition, the online *Decanter*, decanter.com, runs several newsletters and alerts. Its consumer-based fortnightly newsletter has 29,000 readers and the daily news alerts have 11,500 recipients (see Figure 5.10).

Decanter.com recently launched a unique newsletter, the *DecanterTrade*, targeted at the wine trade. It features products seeking representation as well as new product releases. It reaches about 11,500 readers (see Figure 5.11, above).

Online advertising

Both online and offline magazines become the best means for a business to advertise and get known. To support a business, a winery or a wine store, advertising online is also very important. In the first days of Internet, the 'Days of Innocence,' advertisers could use only one format: the banner. Then the formats became more and more sophisticated, up to the moment they were entitled 'rich media.' Now online advertising is more about targeting the right people than thinking about the format of the banners.

Formats: from static banner to rich media

In the prehistoric days of the Internet, the first advertising format was the static banner (see Figure 5.12). The advertiser had to deliver the message with colors and a clever or elegant text.

Then formats became more diverse and sophisticated. Around 2002, the new rage was the skyscraper format, a long vertical banner attracting attention by its size (see Figure 5.13).

Figure 5.12   Static banner published on wineloverspage.com

Source: Courtesy of Robin Garr.

Figure 5.13   Vertical banner on wineloverspage.com

Source: Courtesy of Robin Garr.

On the right side of the screen, there appears a very visible banner for the California Wine Club.

Further on, there is a multiplicity of formats: buttons and squares of all sizes and shapes.

The page below (Figure 5.14) of the News section on decanter.com's web site shows various formats of buttons and banners sold for advertising. The number of those on the decanter.com page shows the success of the online magazine:

Figure 5.14   Example of various advertising formats on decanter.com

The second generation of banner formats included more movement as soon as the Flash technology became available. Pop-ups were very popular as an ad format. As its name suggests, a smaller window popped up in front of the web surfer when the page opened. At first the technology was thought fun and entertaining. When it became wildly and widely applied, it started to annoy web surfers, who then acquired a little piece of software allowing them to block pop-ups on their navigator.

Advertisers came up with new ideas, such as interstitial ads. Interstitials are ads that play between pages on a website, much like a television ad plays between sections of a program.

The battle of the readership

In order to draw advertising to their web site, online publications must be able to show a substantial following of readers as well as know their profile. Advertising is their main source of income, and allows them to offer forums and interesting articles. The main characteristic of the ads is to be related primarily to the wine and food industry. In times of hardship, or when no winery or wine-related industry advertises, some costly sites like the *Wine Spectator* online will run ads from cars or banks – thinking that high income readers like theirs will not mind. But they do – especially the women, who are more and more aware of the wine and food world, and more and more present on the Net.

What kind of readership do those online magazines have? The demographics of the online *Wine Spectator* is 82 percent male and 18 percent female, with an average age of 40–44; 82 percent are college graduates and 72 percent are from an executive, managerial and professional background.

If the *Wine Spectator* is the reference in the United States, the *Decanter* magazine fullfills the same function in the United Kingdom. Decanter.com was launched in 1999. After a rocky beginning, it took off in the early years of this century, and is now widely recognized as a leading online wine magazine. It attracts both consumers and the trade across Europe. The demographics of decanter.com are a lot more diversified than the demographics of *Wine Spectator*:

- 79 percent are male and 21 percent female
- 37 percent live in United Kingdom, 24 percent in United States and 15 percent in mainland Europe;
- 55 percent describe themselves as 'beginners with some knowledge about wine' and 44 percent as 'connoisseurs'
- 20 percent are age 25–34; 27 percent age 35–44; 27 percent age 45–54 and 19 percent age 65–74.

The percentage of young adults (the famous Millennials) is almost the same as the percentage of Baby Boomers. The critical mass of web surfers is in the bracket of 25–44 years old, much younger than the *Wine Spectator* demographics.

The offline *Decanter* has the same kind of profile. Founded in 1975, it covers wines and spirits from everywhere in the world. The editorial content is written from the consumer's point of view, but the magazine is read by both the wine trade and by consumers. The magazine has a print order of 40,000 copies per month, with an international circulation (see Table 5.3).

Table 5.3   Decanter distribution by country

Country	Total	Consumers	Trade
UK	19,800	15,800	4,000
North America	8,500	6,300	2,200
Europe	7,000	4,000	3,000
Far East & Australasia	3,000	1,000	2,000

The readership demographic offline seems to be very similar to the online readership: 41 percent of the readers are under 45 years old.

A winery or a wine-related business willing to advertise in online magazines or web sites has to be aware of the demographics of the site, in order to target and refine its strategy, and to make the best use of its budget.

Cost and Return On Investment (ROI) of such an advertising campaign for a wine business

In the days of Web 1.0, the best brand awareness strategy was through the various formats of banners. How did a wine business figure out the best strategy and the best ROI? Most prestigious estates will advertise on highly regarded web sites such as the *Wine Spectator* or *Decanter*. They might also expand their brand awareness on the site of the major dailies and their special interest pages or newsletters, such as the Food Letter of the *New York Times* or the weekend Food section of the online newspaper. The budget for running such ads is very high.

For example, an American winery A has a site in both English and German languages. Its management wants to increase the visibility of the brand among wine consumers in the United States, the United Kingdom and Germany, where tastings and wine dinners will take place in the spring and the fall. For the United States, there is an extra goal, since the management wants to attract more customers to the wine club (Table 5.4).

For this campaign, the average cost of a visitor to the site is US$ 1.47 – which is very reasonable. It is also possible to calculate exactly the cost for each publication or newsletter to find out which one has the best ROI. For example, Publication 1 in the United Kingdom has an average cost per visitor of US$ 0.50, while Newsletter 2 in the United States, in November, has a cost per visitor of US$1.65. This kind of information is important when working on the next campaign and its budget.[3]

Table 5.4   Raising brand visibility

Month	Country	Title	Format	Impr.	CPM	Clicks
March–May	UK	Publication 1	Button	30,000	US$15	889
March	USA	Publication 1	Exclusive banner	100,000	US$40	1654
March	USA	Newsletter 1	Message + image	30,000 readers	US$18	651
April	Germany	Publication 1	Skyscraper banner	50,000	US$15	952
April	Germany	Publication 2	banner	50,000	US$18	621
September	USA	Publication 2	Exclusive banner	100,000	US$45	2045
Sept.–Nov.	UK	Publication 1	Button	50,000	US$15	934
October	USA	Newsletter 1	Message + image	25,000 readers	US$18	256
November	Germany	Newsletter	Message + image	51,000 readers	US$25	1345
November	USA	Newsletter 2	Sponsoring issue	85,000 readers	US$45	2310
November	Germany	Publication 2	Banner	50,000	US$25	1034
Total					US$18,690	12,691

Online and offline press, as well as pure players in the wine press, show how the trade has answered the challenge of the new technologies through original online magazines and forums. Consumers were then able to find more and more information on brands, the industry and the trade. A more informed consumer generated the side-effect, rather unexpectedly, of the rise of e-commerce. In every country – the United States, the United Kingdom and in continental Europe – e-commerce developed, but did not prosper as rapidly as expected. It is the saga of this difficult industry that we will now recount.

E-commerce: a rocky road

Everybody knows the famous joke: 'What is the best way to make a small fortune in wine? Start with a big fortune!.' This sad joke could apply to many online stores that did not at first succeed, they collapsed but then were revived in a more profitable environment. Why? Up to 2005, less than 1 percent of wine sales occurred online – less than $60 million in sales, when the general wine business generates around US$23 billion.

Table 5.5   Online buying by country

Country	Average no. of purchases online	Average € amount spent
United Kingdom	12.37	1,284
Germany	9.90	594
Denmark	9.31	1,078
Norway	7.14	1,074
France	5.55	374
Sweden	4.90	577
Belgium	4.41	701
Netherlands	3.31	612
Italy	3.17	450
Spain	2.32	522

However, an increase in sales can be expected because e-commerce is becoming more a part of the consuming habit of the average Internet user. Even Europe – generally very much behind the USA or Japan – is spending more money online (Table 5.5).

It is interesting to note that some countries are buying less often but spending more money, that is, Belgium, Netherlands and Spain. Some others are buying multiple small purchases: France and Germany are showing their distrust of the Internet media in this way. The countries with the most confidence in the Internet are the United Kingdom, Denmark and Norway.

How does that translate into the wine business? A recent study, conducted by Prof. Grégory Bressoles from the Bordeaux Management School, and which he presented during Vinexpo 2007, revealed the backstage of wine selling on the Internet and the key success factors of this distribution channel at the international level:

> The online wine market is expanding, exhibiting an annual growth rate of around 30 percent. Following the pattern of other consumer goods, the sale of wine on the Internet is experiencing growing success in France and throughout the world. Although this market still represents a very small proportion of the total market, it is estimated to be worth 100 million euros in France and slightly under 2 billion euros worldwide, that is 5 percent of global wine sales across all distribution channels. In France, more than 200 e-commerce sites share this market. However, three players generate turnover of more than 5 million euros each: 1855.com (€14.7m), Chateauonline.com (€9.4m) and WineandCo.com (€5.5m).[4]

To conduct his study on the online wine stores, Dr. Bressolles created a panel of international Internet users, who had to judge pre-selected web sites using a number of criteria. His table (Table 5.6) is very enlightening.

Table 5.6 Results of Professor Bressolles's panel[5]

		Number of Internautes	Mark / 20	Information (/5)	Offer (/5)	Design (/5)	Ease of use (/5)	Security / Privacy (/5)	Interactivity / Personalisation (/5)	Reliability (/5)
1	www.wine.com (US)	106	15.34	3.84	3.87	3.94	3.97	3.65	3.78	3.80
2	www.nicolas.com	100	14.88	3.78	3.75	3.67	3.85	3.63	3.57	3.79
3	www.Jalthwaltes.co.uk (UK)	100	14.76	3.82	3.84	3.74	3.75	3.55	3.52	3.62
4	www.rouge-blanc.com	101	14.61	3.71	3.69	3.59	3.84	3.62	3.48	3.65
5	www.vintagecollars.com.au (AUST)	101	14.55	3.67	3.68	3.63	3.69	3.43	3.58	3.78
6	www.vin.fr	101	14.26	3.64	3.61	3.35	3.66	3.51	3.39	3.78
7	www.javlnla.es (ES)	101	14.16	3.63	3.55	3.63	3.72	3.35	3.46	3.45
8	www.chateaunet.com	101	14.10	3.47	3.50	3.45	3.62	3.56	3.42	3.65
9	www.chateau online.de (ALL)	100	14.05	3.62	3.59	3.29	3.42	3.56	3.44	3.67
10	www.cave-spirituelle.com	101	13.94	3.50	3.41	3.37	3.67	3.43	3.41	3.60
11	www.chateauonline.fr	102	13.91	3.51	3.57	3.25	3.45	3.46	3.41	3.70
12	www.vinstis.com	101	13.87	3.41	3.58	3.31	3.41	3.44	3.34	3.79
13	www.1855.com	104	13.86	3.67	3.57	3.11	3.32	3.46	3.47	3.65
14	www.chateauonline.co.uk (UK)	100	13.83	3.59	3.54	3.43	3.42	3.37	3.40	3.46
15	www.Jesavourclub.fr	100	13.73	3.47	3.38	3.31	3.53	3.45	3.34	3.55
16	www.vin-online.net	100	13.62	3.44	3.46	3.30	3.59	3.36	3.24	3.46
17	www.vin-fr.com	101	13.60	3.54	3.34	3.30	3.37	3.53	3.25	3.45
18	www.75ci.com	100	13.59	3.48	3.49	3.21	3.36	3.50	3.34	3.41
19	www.vintagaandco.com	100	13.55	3.48	3.36	3.10	3.46	3.43	3.33	3.54
20	www.wineandco.com	99	13.53	3.34	3.44	3.28	3.15	3.49	3.37	3.61
21	www.mondovino.com	102	13.43	3.36	3.35	3.27	3.54	3.29	3.25	3.46
22	www.chateauonline.it (IT)	100	13.43	3.40	3.23	3.35	3.64	3.32	3.29	3.28
23	www.lavinla.fr	100	13.28	3.34	3.36	3.16	3.32	3.42	3.28	3.37
24	www.sodivin.com	100	13.27	3.25	3.15	3.29	3.41	3.35	3.25	3.53
25	www.milleslma.com	100	13.23	3.25	3.21	3.39	3.40	3.32	3.21	3.39
26	www.	94	13.10	3.26	3.28	3.39	3.19	3.17	3.31	3.34
27	www.oovin.com	100	12.79	3.33	3.31	3.08	3.02	3.14	3.26	3.25
28	www.intercaves.fr	98	11.70	2.78	2.82	2.92	2.86	3.09	2.95	3.06

After conducting this research, Professor Bressolles's team was able to identify the best practices for an online wine retailer through seven main criteria:

"1. **Information**:   Describe each wine accurately via an illustrated information card (labels, …). Give details on the different vintage years. Provide flavor ratings (site wine steward and / or independent guides), the characteristics of the soil, a brief description of the land, flavor advice, information on the storage potential of the wine or information on food accompaniment. Offer multilingual support and have an individual marketing approach for each country.

2. **Offer**:   Develop and update the range regularly, Internet users always like to discover new wines and this enables the retailer to generate loyalty. Offer a large range of products with different prices and characteristics. Allow the Internet user to order a single bottle and not an entire case at once. Put in place promotions to stimulate sales.

3. **Design**:   Use multimedia channels to make online retail less dry (videos, animations …). Offer a graphic charter which is sober and consistent with the types of products sold and the positioning of the site.

4. **Ease of use**:   Offer a user-friendly navigation interface. Facilitate the Internet user's research by offering several search options (by price, region, grape variety, colors, occasion of consumption, etc.). Provide an internal search engine. The merchandising techniques applied to the Internet can be used (bringing topics to the forefront by use of "aisle-end displays", etc.).

5. **Security / Privacy**:   Offer various methods of payment and reassure the Internet user at the point of purchase (bank logos, quality seals, …). Allow easy access to the Terms and Conditions of Sale. Provide information regarding the data protection policy (possibility to unsubscribe from e-mailings, …).

6. **Interactivity / Personalization**:   Enable users to contact the site's wine steward (email, direct chat) in order to obtain answers to their questions. Provide videos of the producer's vineyard in order to establish visual contact. Offer a parcel tracking service online. Use direct marketing techniques to get to know the client base better. Via email, direct, rich and inexpensive communication can be established with the customer. Offering personalized newsletters, adapted to the expectations of the users, forms part of this approach. In order to build up loyalty, offer the best customers access to dedicated services (my favorite wines …).

7. **Reliability**:   Indicate the level of stocks in real time. Offer a variety of delivery methods and timescales. Ensure the delivery can be tracked on the site and/or by email so the customer is informed at every stage. Provide efficient and impeccable customer service in the case of breakages, delays in delivery ...'[6]

Those principles were valid for the early stages of e-commerce, but not always applied by the pioneers, who were creating a new road to commerce. The site wine.com was the undisputed winner of Bressolles' e-commerce barometer at the time.

From failure to success: the saga of wine.com

Two visionary men started the online wine business in the United States, Peter Granoff and his brother-in-law Robert Olson. I met Peter through a mutual friend in San Francisco in his beautiful wine store and bar, Ferry Plaza Wine Merchants. When I called him to tell him I was in town for two days and would like to talk to him, Peter answered immediately: 'we could meet for half an hour tomorrow at 1:00 p.m. at my store.' I agreed promptly, knowing he was an extremely busy man. I was sitting precariously on a stool at the bar when I spotted a nice-looking middle-aged man riding a scooter through the Ferry Building. Quite amused I went back to tinkering with my failing tape recorder. To my utter amazement the 'man on the scooter' walked up to me and introduced himself as Peter. After recovering from this initial shock and reassured that my tape recorder was healthy, I got down to business and saw a very sharp businessman still hurting from the failure of his wonderful dream after so many years.

In 1994, when the Net was just emerging as an economic force, Peter Granoff was a wine and restaurant industry veteran, a sommelier by training. Peter's brother-in-law, Robert Olson, was a computer executive at Silicon Graphics, one of the major Internet players in Silicon Valley. Robert thought there was room on the Net for selling a certain kind of product: one that needed a lot of information, had a passionate and geographically diverse following and was limited in production. Peter immediately thought wine solved the equation. By selling wine online, he could offer the consumer access to a lot of wines not easily found in stores, and also provide the consumer with a lot of information about the bottle. It would also allow small producers to bypass the three-tier system and reach more customers.

While Robert worked on the technical end, Peter set off to talk to smaller wineries, whose owners were at first a little afraid of alienating the distributors. When a few commitments had been agreed upon, Peter set up a warehouse and started selling wines online. In January 1995, virtualvineyards.com went online, even before amazon.com, becoming the first online store offering secure online credit-card transactions. The business model was simple: select some high quality wines, offer them for sale on virtualvineyards.com with a clear presentation and receive payment before delivery directly through a credit card. After six months of activity a business angel invested $500,000 in the company. This allowed the company to hire employees, and more investors injected cash into the budding venture.

By 1996 virtualvineyards.com had 50 employees, and had already outgrown several warehouses. Between 1997 and 2000, the company's sales really exploded: between 1996 and 1998, it sold $10 million worth of wine; in 1999 alone, it sold over $15 million. It was during the heady days of the Internet craze: $85 million was injected in virtualvineyards. In 2000, the company bought a little wine portal, wine.com, for $3 million. Peter recollects that it was about that time that Olson and he lost control of the company, which had 'succumbed to the dot-com vortex of ludicrous expectations.'

When investors inject so much money in a company, they expect big returns. Their business model was amazon.com, whose success and IPO enthused all investors and Internet professionals. Unfortunately, it was not the right business model for the wine industry. In 2000 there were talks of a merger with wineshopper.com, its main competitor. The two companies had nothing in common. Wineshopper's main objective was to make as much money as possible and to go public as soon as possible. The site was backed by the venture capital firm backing amazon.com. As David Darlington summed up accurately in his article, 'Wine dot com,' in *Wine & Spirits*, 'wine.com had been founded by industry pros who loved the product they were selling; Wineshopper had been started by industry pros who wanted to cash in on the wine boom.' The merger between the two sites failed, and, in April 2001, wine.com went out of business.

Peter's dream was destroyed, but his integrity was intact. Every client winery either got its money or its wine back. Peter still believes that wine.com could have 'survived with some major restructuring.' But the burst of the Internet bubble exploded his dream as well. Peter took a few months off to recover from the shock and to think about his future. Although he was hurt by the experience, his professional integrity allowed him to get back into the business, and to create Ferry Plaza Wine Merchants with Debbie Zachareas and Bo Thompson in San Francisco.

Wine.com or not wine.com: branding or not branding?

Wine.com was then bought for $9 million by a smaller company called eVineyard.com. The revival of wine.com brought up the very challenging question of the brand name. During the golden years of the Internet, the question raised was of the branding value of names like Amazon or eBay against generic names such as eToys or wine.com. Which one would convey the e-identity (or e-dentity) better? Robert Fisher, a professor of marketing communications at the University of Western Ontario's Richard Ivey School of Business, believed the brand name was right but the execution was wrong, and that the brand was not dead: 'For me, a dead brand is one with no associations. So these brands are with defunct companies, but they may still be valuable because consumers associate good things with them.' Brad Cook, a freelance writer, has discussed the issue of the brand names of a few e-commerce sites in various fields: wine, toys and pets, for example. He interviewed many marketing consultants, CEOs and academics on these topics.

'Wine.com was a very weak brand in the sense that it did not have much awareness in the minds of prospects,' said consultant Al Ries, co-author of the book *11 Immutable Laws of Online Branding*. 'A powerful brand has both awareness and association. BMW means driving, but most people don't know wine.com or what it stands for.'

According to Ries, generic domain names such as wine.com, eToys.com, and pets.com have no value because they do not build a specific association in the minds of consumers. 'The people who started priceline.com wanted a web site name that connoted low prices,' he pointed out.

Not everyone agrees. 'Our brand name has been "in the works" for 3,000 years and we are doing just fine,' countered Peter Ekman, EVineyards CEO. 'My personal opinion is that the brand name is less important than the business concept and the people executing on the plan.'

Jeffery Parkhurst, managing director of brand valuations at Interbrand, had another take on the idea. '[wine.com] is a sin brand,' he said. 'So there's a consumer base of people who want to buy the product. If you're looking for an Internet channel of traffic, it's about owning those keywords.'

Professor Robert Fisher agreed, with some hesitation. 'If you're looking for wine on the Internet, why not Wine.com?,' he asked. 'I think that if people are going on the Internet for the first time and wanted to buy a bottle of wine they would type "Wine.com" [in their browser].'[7]

It seems that Peter Ekman, then CEO of eVineyards and owner of wine.com, was right. Wine.com gained about 5000 new customers every month in 2001–2. The brand awareness of the site kept growing; mostly through a strong reorganization, an aggressive marketing strategy and financial growth between 2002 and 2006. In 2002, wine.com secured its catalog by adding around ten new articles a day. The site also expanded the scope of its articles, covering topics such as accessories, wine cellars, hand-painted personalized bottles and so on. It also partnered a gourmet food store in San Francisco to offer gift baskets with wine. Wine.com marketed the new products through its co-marketing agreements with other online partners as well as through e-mail to its base of more than 500,000 customers.

Before the 2002 holiday season, Peter Ekman printed 200,000 catalogs, mailed throughout November to corporate gift-givers and gift recipients of wine.com orders during the previous 13 months. The 16-page catalog included high-end bottles of champagne, sets of red and white wine, wine accessories and memberships in wine clubs. 'If online businesses focus just on their Web site, I don't think many will reach their potential,' Ekman explained. 'There needs to be something that supports the Web business. The catalog simply is another avenue that lets people explore great wines and consider them as gifts when they are offline.'[8] In 2003, wine.com increased its circulation of the 28-page catalog to 800,000.

In 2004, a new bold move allowed wine.com to diversify its assets. It acquired A.K.A Gourmet, a cataloger of gourmet food and wine gift baskets, and already a key affiliate partner of the site. A.K.A. Gourmet mailed a 24-page catalog twice a year for a total annual circulation of 700,000. The combined databases of wine.com and A.K.A. Gourmet had 650,000 catalog recipients and 450,000 e-mail addresses. This move showed that Peter Ekman wanted to branch out from selling wine and to expand into the food business. It was a wise move, considering all the restrictive laws which, as we have already noted, vary from state to state with regard to the wine business.

At the time of the A.K.A. Gourmet acquisition, Ekman did not hide his desire to acquire more companies to answer the needs of its corporate customers. For the first time, wine.com was in the black and was even able to receive US$20 million from Baker Capital. The new President and CEO of wine.com, George Garrick, used the money to eliminate debts, to upgrade corporate systems, to implement a new personalized web site platform and to fund marketing and CRM initiatives. By then wine.com had a recognizable and recognized brand name and a unique position as leader in wine e-commerce.

In 2006, wine.com was recognized as one of the United States' leading online wine retailers and wine gifting service providers, selling more than two million bottles while evolving its business into a broader-based lifestyle products merchandiser. How did it become such a success? The company attributed its growth to customer insights and refined merchandising promotions. It also multiplied partnerships with other online participants, such as amazon.com in 2006. The primary goal was to boost feeble consumer use of the Internet to buy wine, which has yet to become a major online target. To tempt more consumers to buy online, wine.com would give amazon.com shoppers a one-time discount of $10 on any order of $50 or more, explained Garrick.

The results from all these acquisitions, capitalizations and partnerships are quite outstanding: in 2004, the company posted $32 million in sales – up 45 percent from 2003 – and shipped wine to more than 100,000 customers in 36 states and the District of Columbia. Garrick predicted that wine.com's sales for both 2005 and 2006 would gallop ahead at a similar 40 percent-per-year clip.[9]

Notwithstanding the commercial aspects of its policy, wine.com had also answered all the criteria of usability, CRM and quality required by a good online site such as defined by Professor Bressolles.

A French e-commerce site: rouge-blanc.com

The French wine online store rouge-blanc.com came in at number four on the list of winners published by Professor Bressolles.

Rouge-Blanc.com was created in 1997. Almost bankrupt, it was acquired in 2005 by Wine Passion, but still could not increase its sales. In 2006, the site was totally redesigned to give a very contemporary feel and subtitled 'the wine passion.' The homepage is divided into red squares, each featuring a 'moment': family meals, parties with friends, intimate moments, formal meals, gift ideas etc (Figure 5.15 on next page).

The new positioning puts the categories of wine on the back burner. The marketing director, Patrick Arnal, explained that a marketing study showed that 70 percent of the wine buyers in supermarkets are women. Women are only 48 percent of their 10,000 customers. Therefore, rouge-blanc.com is now targeting women, who are more inclined to buy wine for a special occasion, a party or a meal – not to stock up their cellar.

Figure 5.15   Homepage of rouge-blanc.com

Rouge-blanc.com and the company Wine Passion have a business model that is quite original in the French Internet wine-selling market. They are the only click and mortar web site with a double activity, Business to Business but also directly to consumer, on the Internet. In contrast to their competitors, who often hold very little stock or even no stock at all, they try to keep a 50,000-bottle stock in order to guarantee daily deliveries to their clients.

Their strength in the wine e-business is not, surprisingly enough, their low prices. At an awards ceremony, Alain Guinot, CEO of Wine Passion, said:

> Even if [our clients] are responsive to this price policy, they say that they appreciate above all the clarity, the simplicity and the editorial profusion of our site. It gives them precise information especially thanks to the product sheets and the organoleptic details. The Internet users value our perpetual research for new products coming from talented winemakers already recognized or on the verge of being recognized. They are also sensitive to the diversity of our product range coming from soils of both the Old and the New Worlds.

Since 2006, rouge-blanc.com has been in the black: it has 50 to 100 orders a day – 50 percent in France, 47 percent in Germany and 3 percent in the United Kingdom. The average basket is about €160 per order, all taxes included (about €140 before taxes). The site has about 50,000 unique visitors a month.

Conclusion

Web 1.0 opened the road to a wonderful adventure: reaching wine consumers in various countries and allowing wine consumers to have access to beverages they had never heard about before. Because of the Web – even with its limitations – our sample consumers Ben, Linda, Chandra, Li, Natasha and all their friends were able to talk to each other and absorb a lot of information they had not even imagined existed.

The new Millennium opened bigger doors and avenues to Linda and her peers: the technical tools allowed her to share her tastings and experiences with her friends and peers all over the world. She claimed the right to join in the 'official' discourse of producers, journalists and marketers, and, by so doing, she changed the brands game. Web 2.0 is the key to this world, where the consumers are not the kings – they can lose their power and be dethroned – but they are the masters of the game. Welcome to the twenty-first century!

CHAPTER 6

Web 2.0 and the new millennium: innovative ways for new trends

'We don't believe that five guys sitting in a room should be able to know the right answers compared to the hundreds of people who are out there. We want to hear people's comments.' This statement was made by Kevin Kells, Development Director of consumer packaged goods at Google, to wine industry executives during the Sixteenth Annual Wine Industry Financial Symposium held in Napa Valley on September 18, 2007.

In saying this, Kevin Kells acknowledged the main changes which had occurred between Web 1.0 and Web 2.0. Web 2.0 is the Web of the new millennium with efficient consumer-oriented tools, blogs, communities like YouTube.com, wikis, webcasts, buzz marketing and virtual worlds such as secondlife.com. Virtual places like these welcomed new consumers, and allowed them to express their needs and to make their demands.

The Web, the wine industry and the consumer are changing, but not at the same speed. The consumer is ahead of the industry. The technology is changing faster and faster, giving new ways to the consumer to put pressure on the industry, and to make contact with it and with the brands. Now the brands have to figure out how to get in touch with this selective, over-informed and disloyal customer.

New web communities: Millennials, GenX and women

Web 1.0 provided the users with interactive communities through forums and clubs. These provided users of the Internet with a way of discussing their favorite topics and engaging in lively conversation. The members were mostly male, and the topics male-oriented. They exchanged tasting notes, information on wines and vintners, and shared tips.

An ongoing netnographic study of wine drinkers on various blogs and webcast communities shows that Web 2.0 took the web users a few steps further and attracted new demographics.

How to identify new web consumers: the use of netnography

In her long and very well documented article on netnography, researcher Karen Lee gives a very accurate definition of the technique:

> Netnography, coined from 'ethnography on the Internet,' is an emerging qualitative research methodology adapting ethnographic research techniques to the study of cultures and communities constructed through the Internet. It uses information that is publicly available in online forums to identify and understand the needs and decision influences of relevant online consumer groups. Compared with traditional and market-oriented ethnography, netnography is far less time-consuming and elaborate, and it can be conducted in a manner that is entirely unobtrusive because it uses observations and claims of consumers in a context not fabricated by the marketing researcher.[1]

This netnographic study started when, about three years ago, I noticed a definite switch of Internet users in various wine communities. Along with the traditional male-oriented middle-aged users of a forum, some other communities were emerging, or getting louder, and needed to be studied more carefully. We targeted two types of community: young wine drinkers and women in the United States. First, we noticed young wine drinkers were not very active on the Net, but were very much talked about by the trade. Second, women were very active, but not very much talked about.

Young people – GenX and Millennials: a new wine culture?

Young adults are among the most targeted and desirable wine consumers, but it is a moving community. When I started teaching the 'Wine and Food MBA' at the Luxury Marketing Institute in Paris in 2005, I taught my students that young people in the United States were called the Generation X – aged 21–40. A year later, I had to modify my teaching to explain that there were two generations of young wine drinkers: the Millennials, aged 21–30, and the GenXers, aged 31–40.

As Patrick Dixon pointed out in *Futurewise*, there was the great divide of the new millennium between those two generations. The wine drinkers aged 30 plus had started drinking before it, and they belonged, culturally speaking, to the last century. Millennials started their adult life with the new millennium, and have a new wine culture (or no wine culture).

Oddly enough, they are not very active on the 'Wine Net,' in spite of the fact that they are very computer and Internet literate, even savvy. There is one exception with the community created by Darryl Roberts, founder of the now defunct *WineX* magazine. This saga and adventure that lasted ten years from 1997 to 2007 started because, 'Young people don't drink wine,' and because Darryl Roberts thought he could prove everybody wrong!

In 1986, while vacationing in Napa, he discovered wine and became obsessed. Back in Los Angeles, he looked for a tasting club, wine magazines and wine stores to learn more about his new passion. He was very disappointed; nothing was targeted at his generation. Darryl claimed one had to be over 100 years old to join any tasting club, to be a wine professional, to understand the wine magazines and to be knowledgeable before entering a wine store. So he founded his own tasting group with people of his own age.

In 1993, he moved from Los Angeles to Sonoma. His idea was to launch his own wine magazine targeted at his generation, the Generation X. Remember those days? Every marketer had read Douglas Coupland and was talking about the Generation X, those young adults who loved rap and rock, who had very short attention spans and who cared only about themselves.[2] Be that as it may, Darryl looked for evidence about why 'young people don't drink wine,' and wondered if it was possible to make them change their minds. What he found after three years of research surprised him. '*It's not that young adults aren't interested in wine, it's that the wine industry isn't interested in them*. And that if we give young adults something to relate to, a comfortable, identifiable "place" where they could learn more about wine and how it can become a part of their lifestyle, they'd adopt it, too.'[3] So he launched *WineX*, a trendy magazine targeting young adults. His readership is very representative of the 1990s demographics for a young magazine: 70 percent of the readers are women and 30 percent are men. Magazines, and specifically lifestyle magazines, are read mostly by women, even if women are not the usual audience for wine magazines like *Wine Spectator* or *Decanter*. Further, 80 percent are between 21 and 30, the Millennials of the twenty-first century; 15 percent are between 31 and 40; 70 percent of them have a yearly income over $75,000. Interestingly enough, according to J. Walter Thompson, 21 to 41-year-olds spend 10 percent more on everything compared to those over 41. People in this age demographic pay an average of $16 per bottle, with those aged between 21 and 34 being 84 percent more likely to spend $20 or more for a bottle of wine than those aged 35 plus.

Very early on in his new career, Darryl met an unexpected problem. The wine industry did not understand the magazine. Why? When *WineX* began, wine industry executives belonged to the Baby Boom generation, men in their forties and fifties who, claimed Darryl Roberts, could not understand the culture of the young adults. Having read several issues of the defunct *WineX* with delight, I have to disagree with this comment. The content *can* be understood by Baby Boomers, whether male or female, with a minimal sense of humor, an open mind and a certain culture. On the other hand, from the standpoint of a potential advertiser from the wine industry, the contents of the magazine might have lacked a focus on wine to some extent.

Whatever the reasons, or the reasoning, behind this situation, the fact was that *WineX* did not attract enough advertising to survive in print, and discontinued publication in early 2007. By the end of the same year, however, the magazine was relaunched on the Net with a rather original business model (Figure 6.1). An online version is available for free, there is a newsletter where wines are rated only by points (no tasting notes), called *JustWinePoints Weekly eMail Blast*, and a blog.

The monthly issue itself is conceived as a blog entry. Web users click on 'Current Online Issue' and get to the Table of Contents. By clicking on the page number, they get to the 'article,' and can add their own comments as in any blog.

But is there a real community of young wine lovers around *Wine X*? Judging by the modest number of comments on the blog, it does not look like it, unfortunately. What are the reasons for this situation? It could be due to the very tone of the magazine, which is provocative, derisive and sometimes inflammatory. While the whole purpose of *WineX* is to talk to young wine drinkers, the *JustWinePoints* initiative is counter-productive. What is the point of a rating without any comment on the wine? What are the credentials of the 'grader'? What experience is behind the grading? Why should a reader trust the judgement, and then run to the nearest wine store to purchase a wine just because it has been anonymously awarded 95 points?

Young wine drinkers are certainly looking for something different from the wine business, but it does not seem to be coming from *WineX*. Where

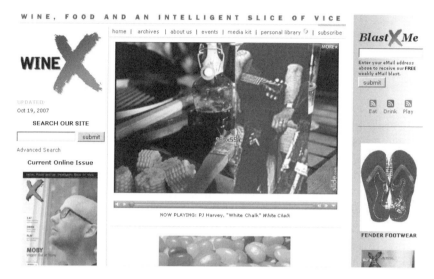

Figure 6.1   Homepage of *WineX*

are they on the Web when the subject is wine? Somewhere else – probably leading communities of wine fans in innovative ventures.

The new www: women, wine and web

On the other hand, women form a very active community on the Net, as the numerous web sites and organizations about women and wine have shown in recent years. Table 6.1, opposite, lists a few such web sites.

Is there a special 'voice' on web sites run by women? Certainly. They are usually about 'lifestyle,' giving, sharing and exchanging tips, and laughing. There are no erudite tasting notes, no comments on vintages and wineries, but portraits of people, charity dinners, fun and laughter. Most of these web sites share the same values:

Wildwomenonwine.   'Wild Women on Wine was created from great friends celebrating and having a tremendous amount of fun and laughter. By simply spending enough time together, it creates opportunities to be open, silly, and share ourselves with each other. What a lovely gift to our friends and ourselves! Because of this time spent with girlfriends, it allows us to give more fully to the rest of the people in our lives.

To be Wild Women on Wine means that you embrace the joy of life and there is lots of fun and laughter in your world and it is filled with

Table 6.1   Some recent web sites founded by women

Site URL	Country	Founder	Date of creation
Wildwomenonwine.com	USA	Cathy Wolk-Nelson Shanin Martin	2000
Womenforwinesense.com	USA	Michaela Rodeno Julie Williams	1990
Femivin.com	France	Isabelle Forêt	1996
Bubblylifestyle.com	France-USA	Carol Duval-Leroy	2007

great friends! You probably love wine, cheese, chocolate, friends, fun, talking, and shopping! Maybe not all, but at least three, probably four to five!'

Bubblylifestyle.com. 'Champagne is part of our lifestyle. Only a woman, especially a woman from Champagne, could create this site and this forum about Champagne and lifestyle. Carol Duval-Leroy is happy to welcome you on this site. Please be sure to share your tips, recipes, travels and stories with us. Enjoy!'

Womenforwinesense.com has a more professional tone because it targets mostly professional women in the wine business. But its specific goal is still to share knowledge of wine: 'Women for winesense is committed to ensuring that all women and men, worldwide, have unbiased information about the cultural, social and health effects of moderate wine consumption, in order to protect the duty and the right of individuals to be responsible for their lifestyle decisions.'

From the United States to Old Europe, it seems that women are more interested either in the festive side of wine or on the professional side of the industry. This spirit helps to create and cement a community. How does it happen?

Bubblylifestyle.com (Figure 6.2 on next page) is one of the leading communities of women interested in wine, lifestyle and food, since the site and the forums are now available in both French and in English. Carol Duval-Leroy is the owner and CEO of Champagne Duval-Leroy, which she has managed since the untimely death of her husband in 1991. The specificity of bubblylifestyle is that it addresses a community of women not only in France, the country of origin of Carol Duval-Leroy, but it also addresses the international community. In French the site is called laviepetille.com (life sparkles), quite appropriately for a site created by a Champagne woman!

Figure 6.2   Homepage of bubblylifestyle.com

Source: Courtesy of Champagne Duval-Leroy.

Figure 6.3   The 'Entertaining' page on bubblylifestyle.com

Source: Courtesy of Champagne Duval-Leroy.

The site offers the possibility of sharing recipes, tips on travel and wine (Figure 6.3). The purpose is to share between women and men everything leading to a pleasant and international lifestyle. Every month bubblylifestyle.com offers new ideas for weekends, new tips on design and parties: joy, pleasure and elegance are the key words of the site.

Is blogging the new PR?

Web communities such as bubblylifestyle.com are very important and popular among men and women – not young people, as we previously saw. Are those young adults more attracted to blogs and blogging? How can we use blogs and blogging to build a community and, in the longer term, a brand? Is blogging the new PR?

First of all, what is a blog and how does it differ from a forum? A forum allows the web surfers to discuss subjects interest between themselves and share opinions, information and ideas. Blogs are a more structured discourse on a subject or around a brand led by one author. Their number exploded about three years ago. Surprisingly, the technology had existed for many years, but had been used sparingly. It all started with the use of personal pages created by individuals to present their professional activity, or, more simply, just to express themselves without any idea of going public. Then some trendsetters used the technology to promote themselves, an idea or a cause, and found a strong following among Internet users. The blog trend was born. There are now millions of blogs around the world, some very famous and popular, others read only by a few followers and many more are just unknown; 1 percent of all blogs gets 80 percent of the audience.

Bloggers, blogging and blogs

Weirdly enough, in spite of their numbers, bloggers are still the minority in the Web world (Table 6.2).

Why did the blog become so trendy? First, it is a fast and cheap way to express yourself, present your ideas, thoughts and feelings to the

Table 6.2   Bloggers on the Web (percent)

50 + yrs	4%
35–49 yrs	3%
25–34 ayrs	3%
18–24 yrs	9%

world, defend a cause or promote a business. It is in some ways the 'electronic diary' of the new millennium. Second, if a blog attracts a good traffic, the author can sell some advertising and make some money. Third, it is a simple way to share knowledge with the world in the true spirit of the initial Net – Wikipedia is possibly the best expression of this ambition. Fourth, and a very important point for business, it is a good way for a brand to test its ideas for new products with consumers and web users, and to start a conversation with its customers or opponents. Last, but not least, the blog is the right place to find other like-minded bloggers, and to start a community around a passion or an individual.

Who is in the audience for a blog? We do not have many tools available to evaluate the audience of the blogosphere. The main and most reliable one is Technorati, which bases its evaluation on the number of links. Other measurement software have different criteria to analyze the audience and the traffic. None of these tools has any way to rate the content of a blog. This situation explains why we have different approaches to the figures, sometimes even contradictory information.

According to Technorati, the first ten most visited wine blogs are English-speaking and come mostly from the United States, with the exception of the South African stormhoek.com blog and the British spittoon.biz blog (see Table 6.3):

Table 6.3   Countries of origin of the top ten wine blogs

1	vinography.com	USA
2	stormhoek.com	South Africa
3	fermentation.typepad.com	USA
4	tv.winelibrary.com	USA
5	wineoutlook.com	USA
6	professorbainbridgeonwine.com	USA
7	drvino.com	USA
8	winecast.net	USA
9	spittoon.biz	UKA
10	lenthompson.typepad.com/lenndevours	USA

What kind of trust do Internet users have in the quality of information delivered by the blogs? According to a very recent study conducted by Nielsen on 27,000 web users in 47 countries, 78 percent of them trusted the recommendation of a peer to buy a product, while 61 percent trusted what they read in blogs.[4]

Blogging for a brand: a new way to link with end-consumers

How can a brand use a blog to its best advantage? Many brands have built a blog in an attempt to get back to the 'top-down messaging' strategy, but the failure of this strategy made marketers and communicators think about finding a better way to use the blog as a participatory communication tool. Blogging is a good way to network. By commenting on other people's blogs, by blogging as well as participating in a wiki, one is building a network of connections between the organization and the audience. These links are very powerful precisely because they can be followed up and commented upon.

The world of wine and food is one of the economic fields where there are many blogs. Among the most famous there is wineanorak.com by the British wine writer Jamie Goode, vinography.com, thewineblog.net, oenoline.com and winecast.net, among many others.

One of the most promising aspects of blogging is the value of direct feedback from users. As we all know, focus groups and panels are very costly to run. The publishing cost of a blog is moderate – mostly accounted for by time and action. The feedback is invaluable – 10 or 20 comments a week on a blog are more valuable because they are unfiltered and less scripted than comments in a focus group. Think about it! Valued customers took precious time out of their workday or their leisure to talk to you and share their thoughts. What could have more value?

The low cost of the technology encouraged Château Beaulieu, one of the oldest Provencal estates, to launch a blog on its new rosé line, Rosé de Provence. What was the purpose? Rosé de Provence is the generic name of all the pink wines in Provence. Legally speaking, Beaulieu did not have the right to name a wine Rosé de Provence, since the term is used by all the estates throughout Provence. Cleverly enough, Beaulieu copyrighted the design of the label, but not the name – opening the door to all its competitors. As good as saying 'Feel free to use the name to promote our wine and our area.' But Beaulieu wanted to hear what the customer and/or the trade had to say on the subject. The blog was open to all, and customers participated in the debate. By taking this step Château Beaulieu showed a good understanding of the mind of the new consumer, 55 percent of whom wanted to be involved in the creation of new products.

Cellar Rat, Ratpack (but no ratatouille):
a new way of winemaking

Some winemakers went even further; they involved end-consumers in the wine-making process. The first initiative in that direction came in 2004 from Crushpad, a luxury winery in San Francisco, California. Crushpad uses grapes from the West Coast's best vineyards, a wine-making team and a winery focused on making wine in small batches. Customers chooses their level of involvement, and Crushpad does the rest. At the end of the wine-making process, customers gets their own 'cult' wine. The customer monitors the wine-making process through a private account, a blog and some videos. Crushpad launched Crushnet, its online wine community, to serve over 2000 Crushpad clients who live in more than 35 states and eight countries. Of course, this initiative has rather a high price.

After three years of work, and with a growing number of members, Crushpad and Crushnet were able to form partnerships with different projects, one of them being with the 'Cellar rat' Alan Baker. Alan Baker took advantage of the Crushnet facilities to launch his own wine-making experience on the Net, the Pinot 2.0 project, made possible by his blog's good following (cellarrat.org), and decided to associate his 'Ratpack' with the experience.

Alan Baker majored in vocal music performance at the University of Northern Iowa, and then worked in Minnesota as a radio producer and technology analyst for 17 years. Becoming bored with his job and having been introduced to *The joys of drinking*, he dramatically changed his life. He quit his job, moved to California and gave birth to the Cellar Rat. Why? Like Darryl Roberts, who we met earlier, Alan had some reservations about the wine industry: 'Over the past five years, I had gotten interested in wine – buying it, tasting it, learning about the winemaking process – but felt like the wine-related media I saw was aimed at an audience I didn't really fit into that well. I read *Wine Spectator*, and TiVo'd Karen MacNeil's PBS show (which is a move in the right direction, accessibility-wise), but I felt like most of the wine press all took themselves very seriously. What I wanted was quirky people with good stories to tell about wine and its place in their lives ... I think the time is right to try and find a way to provide entertaining and informative wine-related media for those who want it.'[5]

Having no experience in wine making, Alan decided he wanted to gain experience by working all the different shifts in a winery for 20 hours a week, and then spend the rest of his time writing his blog and recording interviews. Peterson Winery and Unti Vineyards, both in Sonoma's Dry Creek Valley, agreed to go along with this plan and hired him. Having gained a little experience, he immersed himself in the 'Pinot 2.0' adventure. After the harvest, would-be winemakers were invited to contribute $384 to elaborate a new vintage of Pinot Noir in Mendocino County. Some were able to be physically present, while other investors were too far away to make the trip. They were involved in the experience through the blog and some videos. During the fall and winter 2006/7, Baker and his 50 investors labored at making their first vintage. Instead of writing in his blog, Alan chose to post videos of the work of his crew, under the name 'Ratcast' (Figure 6.4).

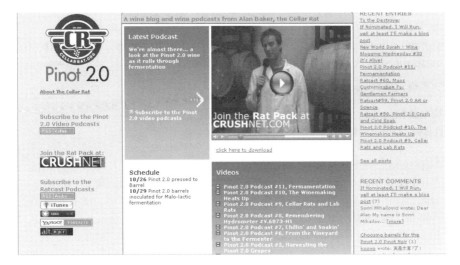

Figure 6.4   Homepage of cellarrat.org

The whole adventure is narrated through videos and interviews. 'I did envision this as a commercial venture,' said Alan Baker, 'and I think it is the first commercial wine produced as a collaboration with a community of wine lovers.' But Baker did have to admit that he will only break even if he sells all the wine.

It is, therefore, too early to answer our question about whether blogging is the new PR. But blogging is certainly a tool that marketers, communicators and academics can add to their tools for good communication. It is also represents a new way of doing things in the marketing department (see Table 6.4).

These are just tips which the marketer can use (or discard). One might agree or disagree with them, but they contain some interesting

Table 6.4   Old and new marketing methods

Old ways	New Ways
Hire a creative advertising agency	Hire a creative user-focused designer
Work with focus groups and panels	Create a blog and listen to users' comments
Print ads	Buzz marketing on the Net
Ads saying how you're better than the competition	Ads showing you learned from the competition
Slick product brochures	Online case studies with real users on your products
Slick company brochures	Participatory web site with a forum or a blog
Promotional newsletters	Online newsletter teaching your readers something
Hire a buzz marketing firm	Create a buzz around something worth talking about
Hire a branding expert	Hire a 'user happiness' expert

topics: authenticity, co-creation and inside-out branding, which are undoubtedly new ways of seeing marketing.

Webcasts: are 'podcasts' the new online news channel?

Podcasts are also a very valuable way of learning what your customers or users think about you. However, we should not use the word 'podcast' since Apple claims to own it, being a contraction of iPod and broadcast. Instead, we will talk about webcasts, audiocast or videocast. Some of these webcasts can be audio files or video files.

What is the best way to promote this new tool?

Webcasts are mostly promoted through syndication. The webcasts are linked together through various sites, and can be played freely by the surfers. They can be presented, for example, on iTunes, brightcove.com hosting the webcasts of the winespectator.com and on the open source site, Get Democracy. They are promoted through the viral channel.

A winery talks to its end-consumers

Like blogs, webcasts are of two types:

- branded webcasts for an estate or a winery
- thematic webcasts – about wine, food, women, travel, lifestyle, etc.

Château Palmer, a Classified Growth in Margaux, launched its blog first, then its webcasts. What is the purpose behind these unusual actions by a very formal Bordeaux estate? The blog was at first intended to replace the 'News' page of the first site. In 2004, when the second version of the site was opened, a blog was quite a novelty. Château Palmer was the first Classified Growth to open a blog, and, as far as we know, is still the only one to have such an interactive tool. The management very quickly understood the use of such a tool: to interact with their consumers and wine lovers. Their posts are open to comment, and whoever wishes to express an opinion is welcome to do so. I do remember the first post on the German blog. A German winemaker living in Provence posted an enthusiastic message, saying how wonderful it was that a French estate would try to reach out to its German customers! That is how, from the very start, the management came to understand that the German market had been taken too much for granted, and had to be worked on. From then on, the German site was even more carefully managed, and the newsletter was always sent in German to the German Club members.

The first webcasts were launched for the 2006 harvest after much thought. Once more Château Palmer was a pioneer in Bordeaux, and, in this usually rather conservative area, the Châteaux owners gave interviews which were then published as a webcast. The site of the *Wine Spectator* is now full of this sort of video.

Until this move by Château Palmer, no estate had published its own webcasts. Harvest is a crucial time for a château, and filming it, as well as interviewing the participants, is rather tricky. Accidents may happen, rain may fall, thunderstorms may occur – and everything will be recorded. Of course one may edit the film or the interview, but then where is the honesty in such an enterprise? The idea is to give the consumer information, which is as accurate and truthful as possible. The risk cannot ever be described as non-existent for a winery. Château Palmer took the risk, and so became famous for the quality and realism of the information given to its customers and web visitors, their famous 'Palmernauts' (from the contraction of Palmer and *internautes*, the French word for web visitors)!

This type of 'branded' webcast is the best way to reach the end-consumers. Life at the Château and interaction with the team are shared with every end-consumer and Club member.

The "voice" of WineLoversPage.com

Thematic webcasts are different. They aim to bring together people sharing a common interest or passion, in our case wine or wine and food.

That is what Robin Garr initiated when, in 2007, at the suggestion of longtime friend Randulo, he launched the WineLoversPage.com Talkshoe, a weekly live Internet radio show.

A wine lover since his first visit to the Napa Valley in the 1960s, Robin Garr wrote a weekly wine column for *The Louisville Times* and *Courier-Journal* from 1980–90. He has written about wine for many publications ranging from *The New York Times* to special-interest magazines, including a regular wine feature appearing in the *Louisville Magazine*. He appeared as 'The Classical Connoisseur' on National Public Radio's Radio Catskill as a regular commentator on food and wine. He has also written extensively about food and restaurants. He was an organizing wine judge at the Kentucky State Fair, and has participated in its judging over two decades. He has also judged wines at Italy's Banco d'Assagio at Torgiano, the Sydney International Wine Competition, Vino Ljubljana in Slovenia, the Indiana State Fair and the Maryland Wine Festival.

Robin Garr has been involved in wine appreciation online since the mid-1980s, serving as a manager of CompuServe's Wine Forum for nearly a decade before the evolution of the World Wide Web. He created WineLoversPage.com (then titled Robin Garr's Wine Bargain Page) in 1994 as one of the first independent wine-education websites, and has presided over its growth into the largest, most popular and most highly awarded wine destination on the Internet. He began its Wine Lovers' Discussion Group, the first web-based interactive wine-appreciation community, in 1996, and he launched the popular email newsletter, *The 30 Second Wine Advisor*, at the start of 1999.

In writing for print and online publications, he has held firm to two core principles. He works to make wine accessible to a wide range of readers, from beginners to experts and wine professionals, and he adheres to the basic principle of 'Straight talk in plain English about fine wine.'

Robin Garr's voice on the Internet is very different from the other journalists coming from the print media to the online world. Through his forum, he created a lively international community of wine lovers and professionals, who, over the years, became acquainted, organized offline dinners and parties and kept sharing discussions, ideas and tips. To maintain and improve the links in his community, Robin took advantage of the new technological tools and learned how to use them to the benefit of his site and the community. The webcast is one of them.

Robin's show is hosted on the talkshoe.com platform (Figure 6.5), which is a community of web users and show hosts.

This page shows the webcasts currently on the platform. The categories are on the left. Robin's webcast is hosted in the Food and Spirits section (Figure 6.6):

Figure 6.5 Sample page from talkshoe.com

Figure 6.6 Homepage of talkshoe.com

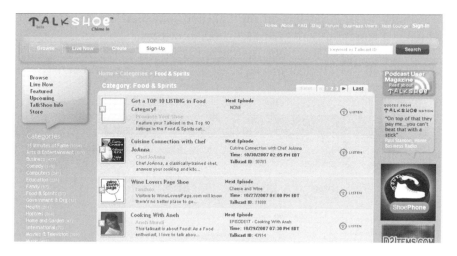

Figure 6.7   WineLoversPage.com/ Talkshoe page

Because of its success, the 'WineLoversPage TalkShoe' is rated number three among the 37 wine and food shows (Figure 6.7) in the talk-shoe platform's top list of top shows (at the end of October 2007). Robin advertises his talk show on his own website.

How does it work? Every week Robin suggests a topic related to wine: for example, how to read a French label, corkscrew or screw-cap, unusual wine and food pairings, wine goes to Hollywood, Champagne or Burgundy, wine and cheese, and so on. The audience can listen to the live show, call in to give an opinion or take part in the topic, or download the show after it is completed.

Webcasts are not only videos or audio interviews. Behind the scenes there is a syndication technology called RSS requiring skills in programming and editing, which were provided by Randulo. The technology allows much better interaction with the web users. People can talk to the show host live and/or can download the webcast – keeping it for further listening on their MP3 or iPod at a convenient time.

Webcasts, like blogs, are syndicated and have a life of their own on the Net. Once they start being syndicated they reach more and more people. Robin Garr thinks each of his webcasts are downloaded at least 500 times, which is a very good rate.

Crushpad and WineLibraryTV:
to get more than the bottle of wine

'Wine lovers increasingly want more than the bottle of wine itself; they want an immersive experience and to participate in something bigger than themselves,' said Crushpad President, Michael Brill, in his press release dated August 30, 2007. To allow wine lovers and enthusiasts 'to get more than the bottle,' Crushpad joined up with Gary Vaynerchuk, the founder and leader of the WineLibraryTV blog and webcast.

In spite of his young age, Gary is now a star of the Internet wine business. Director of Operations at Wine Library in Springfield, New Jersey, Gary started a love affair with wine by reading the *Wine Advocate* by Robert Parker and tasting all kinds of wines when traveling. Like a lot of young men of his generation, such as Darryl Roberts and Alan Baker, Gary grew dissatisfied with 'the stuffiness of the industry-conceited sommeliers, snobby shopkeepers unwilling (or unable) to educate their consumers, and seemingly mystical conventions all combine to make wine seem intimidating to the uninitiated,' as he explains on his website. WineLibraryTV was born because Gary wanted to show that wine can be (and is) fun. His videos are full of spin and humor but address all the important issues of wine – tasting wines, how to train your palate, the importance of oak and barrel aging in creating 'monster wines' – to name just a few.

By the end of 2007, Gary Vaynerchuk had a following of 30,000 weekly video webcast viewers. He has just had a new idea to both cement his community of wine fans, dubbed the 'Vayniacs' (Figure 6.8), and to take them beyond consuming and collecting wine to creating their own 'Vayniac Cab' (Cabernet Sauvignon).

Gary and Crushpad worked together to source the grapes, provided guidance for the wine-making team and are now in the process of aging the wine. The Vayniacs can participate in the process by pre-buying one bottle of the luxury and exclusive Cabernet Sauvignon (the price is not publicly released). The largest purchasers will be invited to participate in the final blend. Every Vayniac will be invited to the 2009 release party.

The creation of the Vayniac Cab is the next level of involvement for web users and wine fans. 'With the Vayniac Cab project,' said Gary Vaynerchuck, 'we'll expand on that idea by putting thousands of wine lovers in the middle of it all simultaneously, to experience the fun and make an insanely great wine in the process.' The Vayniacs interested in the experience 'can track the progress' on videos posted on the WineLibraryTV site (Figure 6.9).

Figure 6.8   WineLibraryTV – Vayniac Wine

Source: Courtesy of Wine Library.

- Track the Progress

   * Join the Vayniac Cab group on Crushnet, where you can track the progress of the
     grapes, view video of all the Vayniac madness in the trenches, and discuss the wine with
     other Vayniacs.

Direct any and all questions about this project to our Crushpad liaison, Stuart Ake:
stu@crushpadwine.com

Figure 6.9   Vayniac podcast

Source: Courtesy of Wine Library.

Since the experience is still ongoing, we invite readers to stay tuned to tv.winelibrary.com!

A rat with a 'long tail': wine brands and online retail

Chris Anderson's book on the 'Long Tail' of the book and music business triggered the interest of British retailer, Edwin Booth, manager of the wine store everywine.co.uk (Figure 6.10).

What is the idea behind *The Long Tail*? Everybody has heard about the 20/80 rule: 80 percent of income comes from 20 percent of customers. In real life, in the book industry you have bestsellers; in music, hits; and in movies, blockbusters. The virtual world changed this rule. In a virtual catalog, 98 percent of the available products sell at least once a year. Anderson took the music industry as an example, offering downloads of songs on the Internet, and put the curves in a on a graph:

> It started like any other demand curve, ranked by popularity. A few hits were downloaded a huge number of times at the head of the curve, and then it fell off steeply with less popular tracks. But the interesting thing was that it never fell to zero. I'd go to the 100,000th track, zoom in, and the downloads per month were still in the thousands. And the curve just kept going: 200,000, 300,000, 400,000 tracks ... there was still demand ... In statistics, curves like

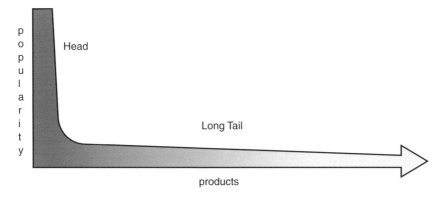

Figure 6.10   'The Long Tail'
Source: Resmo.

that are called 'long-tailed distributions' because the tail of the curve is very long relative to the head.[6]

Wine cannot be downloaded like a song or a video, but it can, however, be bought online like a book. Like the book industry, too, a few international brands are controlling the territory, but there are also tens of thousands of other brands or wines still available in the market. These wines are bought from time to time by wine lovers who are more adventurous or more experienced than others. They are the 'long tail' of the wine business and still bring in money.

Edwin Booth applied the business model of amazon.com to his online wine store. 'Working on consignment,' explains journalist Robert Joseph in *Meininger's Wine Business International Magazine* (October 2007), 'has enabled Booth's everywine.co.uk to offer its consumers 44,173 different wines without costing him a penny in stock.' Even better, 'if you google an obscure wine name such as Favorita from Italy, or a small Burgundy winegrower, everywine's name will come up, largely because Booth has put the emphasis on search engine optimization. Winesearcher.com lists over 37,000 of everywine's products.' It is a huge success for Edwin Booth. His business is 'all tail and no head,' as he stated. 'The last 8,500 wines we added to the site,' explains Edwin to journalist Robert Joseph, 'represented 18 percent of July's [2007] orders.'

If, economically speaking, this business model is a success, how does the good word spread over the Internet? Word of mouth or buzz marketing is a good tool when applied to the wine business. Indeed, consumers are now not only a target but also part of the media themselves.

Buzz marketing: who or what is the most efficient bee buzzing on the Internet?

'Word of Mouth,' 'Viral Marketing,' 'Buzz Marketing' – all these phrases cover well-known offline marketing strategies now developed and applied to the Internet. There are many types of buzz marketing, some of which apply to the wine business. We have already studied a few cases, like the building of communities, but three main areas remain unexplored in the wine business: the content-oriented buzz, the user-generated content and the influence buzz through trendsetters, also called 'influencers' or 'community leaders.'

Content-oriented buzz:
'it is about WHO you know'

Many initiatives in Europe and in the United States, two mature markets, use the content-oriented buzz to generate more business, or, even better, to create an innovative strategy. This is the case of the Club WineWeb launched in October 2007 in the United States by Ron Kreutzer, President and Founder of WineWeb Enterprises Inc (Figure 6.11). His company already provides The WineWeb^{TM}, an e-marketplace that maintains a directory of over 34,000 wineries from all over the world, and has over 100,000 wines available from the wineries and online wine merchants. Ron Kreutzer took the idea of the wine club a step further than the wine club generated by the Web 1.0. Club WineWeb, his new venture, differentiates itself from the wine clubs of Web 1.0 by two characteristics:

- It offers wines direct from small-production wineries, whose high-quality wines are not available in stores or require one to be on a waiting list to get an allocation;
- It is an invitation-only club: the potential member must have received an invitation code from a current club member, or been given the invitation code at a WineWeb-sponsored event.

Figure 6.11   Club WineWeb

One could wonder if such an idea is counter-productive. 'We want to promote viral marketing and word-of-mouth marketing in a wine club,' said Ron Kreutzer to emediawire.com on October 6, 2007. 'It also provides another marketing channel for our clients' wines.' Will the site be able to sustain itself with only a word-of-mouth strategy? Club WineWeb will offer wines so incredibly good that customers will recommend it to their friends and make a success of it: 'Our success will be dependent on offering wines that you want to tell your friends about,' claims the blurb on the homepage of the new site.

This idea of private clubs relying on word-of-mouth from consumers is rather trendy on the Internet at the moment. In France, two wine clubs were born in 2007 on the same principle. Cave-privee.com (private cellar) was founded by Benjamin de Longuerue, former Marketing Director of the online store, chateauonline.com. It is also an invitation-only club.

Like its American counterpart, cave-privee.com (Figure 6.12) selects highly sought after and exclusive wines at a good price. Each member receives a mailing with the new offer and can forward it with a recommendation to a friend and/or buy the wines. After less than a year of business, cave-privee.com has a fairly good number of members (not disclosed).

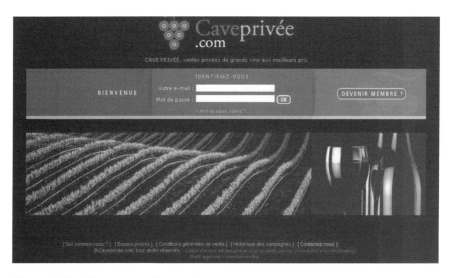

Figure 6.12   Homepage of cave-privee.com

User-generated content:
let the consumer be the author

Some wineries went even further than using the consumer as a tool to get new clients. They allowed or requested their trusted consumers to generate the content of a site, a blog or even create a new product. The most elaborate technology in this field is the 'wiki,' of which wikipedia. org is the prime example.

Looking for a specific wine on the Internet can be a fiddly and time-consuming job. The site wine-searcher.com is a very good tool to find the availability of a wine near one's home, but what if one is just looking for a wine to match a dish and do not have any particular idea? Now one has a new resource, a free wiki wine rating site to find the best wines in a specific location (Figure 6.13).

The idea came up when three people, Jeff Dracup, Colleen Wagner and Kevin Jackson, who enjoy trying new wines, found out that most wines had no rating. 'We felt the 100-point wine rating system, used by Wine Spectator and others, fell short in many respects. First, the ratings come from a select group of people who may or may not have the same taste in wine as the average consumer. Second, and more importantly, there are just too many wines being released each year for all wines to be rated by such a small group of wine tasters,' said Jeff Dracup in his press release (September 6, 2007, published on pr.com). With that statement, Dracup shares the opinion of Kevin Kells, quoted at the beginning of this chapter, who has even gone a little further: 'Who is this "critic" to tell me what I should or shouldn't like? On the other hand if a group of independent consumers say they liked a wine – it is more likely I'm also going to enjoy that wine. I feel more confident buying a wine recommended by many other wine consumers than just a few critics.'

And there we have it, Q.E.D.! Web 2.0 is about user-generated content, and the wiki created by Dracup and his friends is now available. WineApe.com allows visitors to rate wines easily and to find wines based on rating, price or the place sold.

Once the wines have been rated and tasted, the visitor can search the base by type of wines, places to buy or ratings (Figure 6.14).

The three founders of the site respect the privacy of the user, but if a user wants to be notified when a specific wine is rated, he can get an email with the rating. They also use the users' ratings to inform the wineries. 'We're hoping these emails will provide wineries with the feedback from consumers necessary to help wineries improve their wines and offer better wine values,' says Colleen Wagner, President.

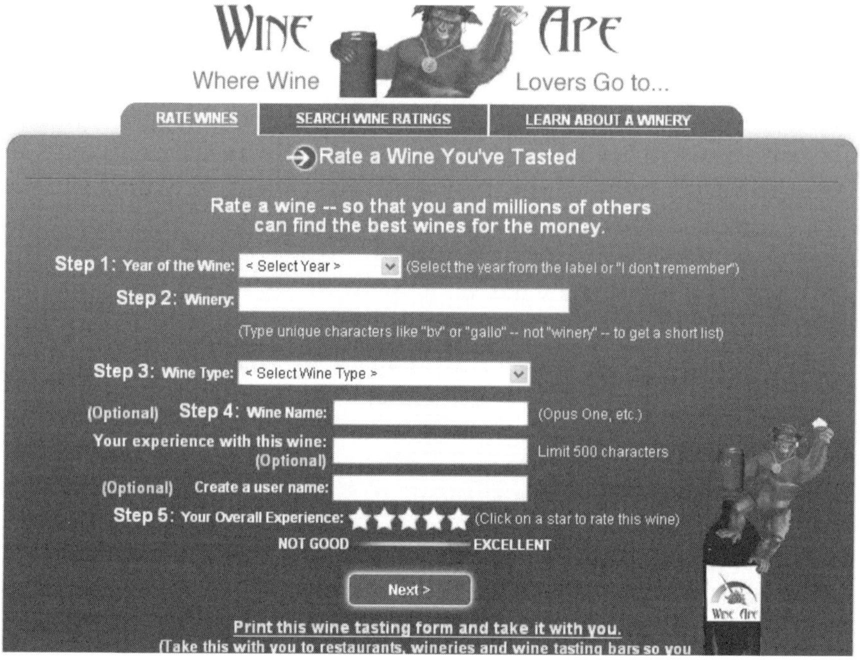

Figure 6.13 Homepage of WineApe.com

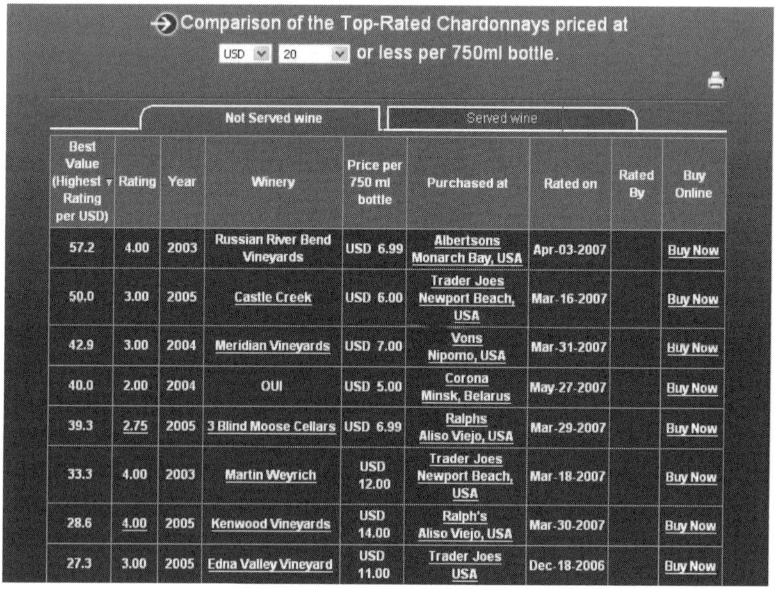
Comparison of the Top-Rated Chardonnays priced at USD 20 or less per 750ml bottle.

Not Served wine | Served wine

Best Value (Highest Rating per USD)	Rating	Year	Winery	Price per 750 ml bottle	Purchased at	Rated on	Rated By	Buy Online
57.2	4.00	2003	Russian River Bend Vineyards	USD 6.99	Albertsons Monarch Bay, USA	Apr-03-2007		Buy Now
50.0	3.00	2005	Castle Creek	USD 6.00	Trader Joes Newport Beach, USA	Mar-16-2007		Buy Now
42.9	3.00	2004	Meridian Vineyards	USD 7.00	Vons Nipomo, USA	Mar-31-2007		Buy Now
40.0	2.00	2004	OUI	USD 5.00	Corona Minsk, Belarus	May-27-2007		Buy Now
39.3	2.75	2005	3 Blind Moose Cellars	USD 6.99	Ralphs Aliso Viejo, USA	Mar-29-2007		Buy Now
33.3	4.00	2003	Martin Weyrich	USD 12.00	Trader Joes Newport Beach, USA	Mar-18-2007		Buy Now
28.6	4.00	2005	Kenwood Vineyards	USD 14.00	Ralph's Aliso Viejo, USA	Mar-30-2007		Buy Now
27.3	3.00	2005	Edna Valley Vineyard	USD 11.00	Trader Joes USA	Dec-18-2006		Buy Now

Figure 6.14 WineApe's page on Chardonnay

Not only does the consumer do that job, but he also enables commercial enterprises to found new business on the strength of their work. 'As people from around the globe continue to enter wine ratings, we hope WineApe will become a valuable source of information to consumers and to the wine industry worldwide,' concludes Tom Duffy, an investor.

Influence buzz, influencers and wine: the new buzz marketing

To conclude our study here is a profile of the 100 percent Internet-oriented consumers: the influencers or trendsetters buzzing all over the Internet.

Who are these 'influencers'? Usually they consider themselves as experts in certain areas such as their work, hobbies or interests. They are very often asked their opinion on some products or services. When they find a product or a service they like, they recommend it to friends. They usually have a large social circle, and are very active online through blogs, forums, emails and social networks.

How do they get their information? They are big information and advertising consumers. While they follow advertising on the Internet, they might not check on the link but will go back to the site to get more information. They cite the source of their information, share it with friends and family, and give their advice on consumers' websites or forums after their purchase.

Influencers are very important to brands that are using their social networks to promote their product. A very intelligent use of the influence buzz was made by the South-African winery, Stormhoek. Stormhoek is a very small winery that hired a blogger and designer, Hugh MacLeod, to promote its wines. MacLeod offered a bottle of wine to any blogger over 21, and with at least three months experience in blogging, who would contact him. They were not under an obligation to mention the wine on their blogs. After six months, more than 100 bloggers had mentioned the wine and published tasting notes on their blogs all over the world. MacLeod then organized 100 dinners in the United Kingdom, Spain and the United States, attracting potential customers interested both in wine and in the technology. The results have been very positive. Sales expanded from 50,000 cases a year to 300,000. Even better, Microsoft asked Stormhoek to create a special wine for its 79,000 employees in 102 countries – the Blue Monster reserve wine – launched in a bar in London's Soho (Figure 6.15).

Figure 6.15   Microsoft bottle

In his blog, MacLeod explains the origins of the project. 'The wine is not a commercially available product, just a wee 'social object' for geek dinners and people inside the Microsoft ecosystem. Microsoft's Steve Clayton and I are still working on the final details of how we're going to get the wine to people who want it, but for now, we're just limiting its availability to (1) people who belong to the 'Friends of Blue Monster' Facebook group, and (2) geek dinners we're attending and/or sponsoring.'

The Stormhoek project is the perfect example of what an influencer like Hugh MacLeod can generate in interest and added value to a project – financially, socially and personally.

Mobile marketing

Is the scenario the same with mobile marketing? While widely used in Japan, mobile marketing is still a novelty in the Western world. Despite this, an American company recently launched a real-time in-store mobile food and wine pairing, eWine Match.

The mind behind eWine Match is chef and wine educator Jerry Comfort, who helped to develop a database grouping foods and wines according to intensity of flavors and reactivity. How does it work for the consumer? The shopper texts the meal's key ingredient or type of cuisine to 411511 and within seconds receives three wine selections. The service is free, is totally portable and responds specifically to the food submitted. 'And the beauty of a data-driven platform,' said chef Jerry Comfort, 'is that it is constantly growing and as we get new and unusual text messages we will continue to expand the database.'

And what a pleasure for the consumer not to have to stand in a supermarket aisle looking in desperation at miles of shelves packed with unknown (or too well known) wines just before dinner time!

Conclusion

From Web 1.0 to Web 2.0, consumers, the wine industry and the trade have come a long way. The consumers went a little faster than the trade and the wine brands. They took over as much space as they could on the Web. Brands are now trying to respond to this demanding and difficult consumer. Do these new tools help to build a good name for a brand, whether a new one or an older one? If they do, how do they help wine brands? And what is a wine brand?

CHAPTER 7

Wine and branding

In seventeenth-century England, in London, the Frenchman François Auguste de Pontac opened the tavern 'L'Enseigne de Pontac,' known as 'The Pontacks,' to promote his wine, the Pontac 'claret.' M. de Pontac was the owner of a wine estate in Bordeaux, in a place called Haut-Brion, which means 'on a hill.' He was the heir to a long tradition in Bordeaux. He lived the luxurious life of the aristocracy in his beautiful château but also had a good head for business. He understood the importance of the English market early on in his life, and spent a lot of time in London, at the Court and among his peers, promoting the Pontac claret. Eventually, as its renown grew, the name of the Estate – Château Haut-Brion – came to replace that of its owners, Pontac. This was in 1663, and the first wine brand was born!

Wine brands: some statistics

Since those days, many things have changed and the number of brands have exploded. Newcomers in the wine business such as Australia, New Zealand, the United States, Argentina and Chile have launched several thousand brands, and now compete in the major consumers' markets, namely the United States and the United Kingdom, the largest being the United States. The United States alone has the largest wine market in the world: 7000 names from France, Italy, Australia, Chile, Spain – in addition to American wines – compete with each other: 96 percent of those 7000 names sell less than 100,000 cases in a total market of 246 million cases.

In the United Kingdom a few brands also dominate the market, as Table 7.1 shows.

This domination of the market by a few names is due to large advertising expenditures that are part of an established and powerful marketing strategy.

But is there really such a thing as a brand in the wine business? It is a very controversial question. In his article 'The Two Cultures,'[1] Jamie Goode insists that wine 'doesn't suit brands.' Most marketers disagree,

Table 7.1   The ten best-selling brands in the United Kingdom and their advertising budgets (2001)

Brand Name	Owner	Country	Advertising budget £
Gallo	E&J Gallo	USA	1,634,834
Jacobs Creek	Caxton	Australia	5,915
Stamps	BRL Hardy Wine	Australia	n/d
Lindemans	Southcorp Wines	Australia	19,032
Banrock Station	BRL Hardy Wine	Australia	272,629
Blossom Hill	UDV Guinness	UK	419,140
Nottage Hill	BRL Hardy Wine	Australia	n/d
Penfolds	Southcorp Wines	Australia	168,588
Stowells	Constellation	UK	978,029
Rosemount	Southcorp Wines	Australia	36,031

convinced that branding is important for all industries, and might even be a matter of survival for the wine industry. According to Professor Vincent Grimaldi, an expert in change management, 'The wine industry – under the spur of cutthroat competition and an excess of supply – is indeed ripe to embrace brand management, and some contenders are already doing it superbly.'[2]

Branding or no branding? That is the question

Jamie Goode in defense of estate wines and terroir

In Europe building a brand is considered a betrayal of the roots of the wine – the famous *terroir*. This is Goode's position in his long and controversial article, 'The Two Cultures,' published in November 2002.

Goode makes a clear difference between 'commodity wines' and 'terroir wines.' 'Commodity wine,' he says, is 'an inexpensive wine purchased … not for its intrinsic qualities but because it serves a purpose, like milk, sugar, or instant coffee.' 'Terroir wines' have geographical roots and cultural links to the place where they were born. He also singles out 'estate wines,' 'made from grapes from a fairly narrowly defined patch of ground' and 'usually owned by the producer.'

To summarize his position, he publishes an interesting table (see Table 7.2) of the characteristics of the two cultures.[3]

Table 7.2   Examining the characteristics of the two wine cultures

Branded wines	Estate wines
• Production is scaleable	• Made from grapes grown in one vineyard, or several neighboring vineyards
• Typically made from bought-in grapes	• Vineyards supplying the grapes are usually owned by the company making the wine, or are supplied by growers on long-term contracts
• often 'international' in style, lacking a sense of place	• Limited production, subject to vintage variation
• Usually defined by winemaking style	• Typically display regional influences or a 'sense of place'
• Made to a style and to fit a price point because production limited only by the supply of suitable purchased grapes, these wines are often widely available	• Availability is sometimes a problem, because of the limited production
• Heavily marketed	• Marketing is often minimal
• Lack diversity	• Hugely diverse

Even worse than the mere technical differences shown above, Goode believes brands to be 'parasites and mimics.' 'Estate bottled wines from famous regions have established wine as a drink with association of class, elegance and sophistication. The wine brands are cashing in on this image that has taken hundreds of years to build, by marketing themselves as 'lifestyle' products that offer this tradition and sophistication.'

Nonetheless, one has to recognize that wine brands can be very good. Think of Penfold from Australia, Champagne from France. Brands have also made a tremendous improvement in the quality of the inexpensive wines and given the consumers consistency of taste and quality. Consumers know exactly what they get when buying a brand they trust.

So what is wrong with branding wine? 'Wine is different to most other drinks in that it is primarily an agricultural – not a manufactured – product. It doesn't suit brands,' Goode states.

We agree with that statement, but not with the conclusion. Indeed, wines as defined by Goode are elaborate cultural products: *terroir*, history, wine making, very often a family behind the wine. This is a little scary for the beginner: could not a brand be Step 1 to a beginner? Goode writes: 'branded wines offer an easily accessible route through the complex world of wine.' Consider this: before writing and reading, all of us went through the painfully long and difficult process of learning our vowels and consonants, then moving on to words, and then to full sentences. We finally upgraded to books, and sometimes complex books. Some of us favor romance, detective stories or magazines while others are comfortable with history books, poetry or philosophy. What is wrong with that? Cannot good and consistent brands be the first step for a young wine drinker or a beginner? Ben and Linda, our sample wine drinkers, will then move on to more sophisticated wines after taking some tasting classes or talking to their peers. They might even end up appreciating the sophisticated European wines. But if, after some tastings, Ben and Linda keep buying wine brands, why should it be held against them or the industry?

Why brand a wine?

It is true that the wine industry and branding do not make easy bedfellows. Some brands, like Postillon or Damoy in France, Blue Nun in England or the Gallo Cream Sherry jug, have disappeared from the shelves, or are now synonymous with entry-level wines. But others replaced them and caused branding, like consumers, to evolve over the years. Since 1995, brands have moved up the quality ladder, led by the Australian and American industries along with the first symptoms of the wine crisis in Europe. This change reflects the shift which the New World producers have brought about in the wine world. While French labels remain challenging for anyone who is not a wine specialist, the New World producers have invaded the American and British markets, and are looking at continental Europe. A branded wine is more easily recognizable by the wine drinker because it is consistent in quality and taste.

What makes European wines so difficult for the inexperienced wine drinker is the constant variation from one year to another. European wines, being 'terroir' wines, are subject to changes in weather, in quantity and in taste. Most European wines are blends of various grapes, with the exception of Burgundy which produces Pinot Noir and Chardonnay wines almost exclusively. But Burgundy is divided between thousands of local producers and 'climates,' making choices even harder. To make things even more difficult, local legislation in Europe usually prevents the mention of the grape variety on the label if it is in a Controlled Appellation Area.

How should a wine be branded?

Let us now examine the other side of the coin: the brands and the process of deciding if a wine should be branded. What is a brand in the wine business? It may be linked to:

- **A place**. A location such as a country (France, Spain, Italy, Australia, Chile, Argentina) or a region (Amalfi Coast, Piedmont, Priorato, Champagne) or a *terroir* (Chassagne-Montrachet in Burgundy, France, Le Mesnil-sur-Oger in Champagne, Santa Rita Hills in California).
- **A grape**. The famous and famed Cabernet Sauvignon, the ever-present Chardonnay, the fashionable Pinot Noir, the popular Pinot Grigio or the Syrah, also known as Shiraz, the Californian Zinfandel, the Italian Sangiovese, among thousands of others.
- **A lifestyle image**. Elegant for expensive wines, such as French Champagnes; casual with a cool rosé wine for a barbecue or a picnic; a nice white wine for a gathering with friends or a nice red wine for a family dinner during the winter.

What are the considerations a marketer should take into account to answer the 'when' and 'why' questions?

Branding decision	Should a Brand be Developed for this wine?
Family brand	Should the brand be individual or family-branded?
Brand extension	Should other wines be given the same brand name?
Multibrand decision	Should 2 or more brands be developed in the same wine line?
Brand positioning	Should the brand be positioned?

The way to arrive at the answers is to know exactly what is expected from a brand. From the winemaker's point of view, a good brand has to offer a concept simple enough to be understood by the consumer, has to target a certain type of consumer and has to carry a good image. The success factors of a brand are:

- knowing exactly what the consumer is expecting: product, packaging, price
- a clear positioning of the product: image

- effective marketing actions: names, web sites, store facings, advertisements

The consumer expects a wine to have a consistent taste and a good quality, to be clearly identified as a type of wine (grape, country) and for the price to be constant.

Key factors for a successful branding strategy

A striking label to 'grab' the consumer's attention?

The first thing a potential buyer sees on a store shelf is the label. A label goes far beyond a single name. Successful wine packaging communicates the individuality, quality and value of the wine to both trade and consumer, from cork to capsule and from print to online communication.

Europe is famous for its austere and incomprehensible labels (Figure 7.1). Those labels are testimony to a long and prestigious history, to a beautiful estate and a gorgeous country.

It is of course very different in countries where the wine industry is more recent. Labels can be fun and humorous. Next to the traditional

European labels with their châteaux and landscapes sit 'funny' labels like Yellow Tail, of course but also French Rabbit, Fat Bastard, Mad Dogs and Englishmen, Glamour Puss, Red Rover (Figure 7.2), Hocus Pocus or Wild Pigs.

Other labels are more feminine or 'cute,' like the RoseEros or A rose is a rose is a rose (Figure 7.3) created by Château Beaulieu in France.

The goal is to be different. If one remembers that 7000 brands are competing in the United States alone, one will understand why differentiation is such a mandatory feature for a brand. But for one wine brand to be different from

Figure 7.1 Sassicaïa label

Figure 7.2   Red Rover label
Source: Resmo.

Figure 7.3   A Rose is a Rose label

another is not enough in such a competitive market. A brand needs what Marty Neumeier, author of the *Brand Gap*, calls 'radical differentiation.'

The differentiation might be adequate and meaningful in the market where the brand originated, but can become meaningless in some targeted markets. Yellow Tail or French Rabbit are unimaginable in the Chinese or Indian markets, but Château Palmer is very well received in Asia. Why? There is no cultural reference in the Asian wine market to funny or humorous labels. Wine is still taken very seriously and is a status symbol.

In mature markets which are saturated by a wide variety of labels, funny or cute labels are for the most part more suitable. They help customers to memorize the brand. If the name escapes Ben or Linda when shopping, they will catch sight of the funny label on the shelf. The traditional naming process – a place or a visionary ancestor perhaps – is no longer adequate.

Studies have shown that most people cannot remember the name of the wine they drank the night before. It is particularly critical in restaurants where the customer cannot hold the bottle and has to refer to a wine list. He will have a choice between Château Something,

Figure 7.4   Kono Baru label

Figure 7.5   Clarendelle rosé label
Source: Courtesy of Clarence Dillon Wines.

Figure 7.6   Tapeña label
Source: Tapena.

Something Valley or Something Creek, but will settle on Laughing Stock or Glamour Puss. The waiter will then chime in and sing the merits of the wine. Bottle sold!

How can one forget the upside-down label of the Kono Baru wine (Figure 7.4), launched by Three Loose Screws, a division of Don Sebastiani and Sons, or the serigraphed silver label of Clarendelle rosé (Figure 7.5) or the roughly-drawn, screen-printed white outline of a fork painted on the bottle of the Spanish Tapeña brand (Figure 7.6)?

Is there a meaning to these labels? You bet there is! The upside-down label of Kono Baru means that the wines come from Southern Australia – the other part of the world down under. But the meaning goes even further, according to Donny Sebastiani, marketing director of Three Loose Screws, who told journalist Mary-Colleen Tiney of *Daily News Links* (May 4, 2007). 'You really have to grab the consumer … The label is meant to set ourselves apart because there's no reason for the consumer to look for a new brand. Nobody's walking into a store hoping for a new label to buy.'

That might be why the creator of Clarendelle, Robert de Luxembourg, opted for a special label and name. The name itself was inspired by the name of his grandfather, Clarence Dillon, and is meant to be understood and pronounced easily in various languages. The label design is meant to differentiate the rosé wine, an easy summer drink, from its more serious 'brother and sister,' the red and white Clarendelle.

Tapeña, a Spanish Tampranillo, owes its name to the famous 'tapas,' those little snacks you eat in Spain. Tapeña is the friendly wine to go with the food.

The shape of the bottle

A label has to carry some meaning for the consumer, and have a story behind it. Without that, the producer is unlikely to have much success selling his wine.

The second component of packaging is the bottle. Shape, color, foil and cork or screw-cap all play a vital role. The spirits industry is more imaginative than the wine industry in shaping the bottle: the peculiar form of the Grand Marnier bottles, the spectacular shape of some Cognacs and the elegant bottle of the Suze liqueur. While the wine industry is no match for the spirits industry, wine producers are bending over backwards trying to be unique, to be different from each other.

In the wine business shaping the bottle is considered less important than designing a fancy label, and that could be a mistake. An easily recognizable shape is a good marketing argument. Look at the story of the Château Haut-Brion bottle (Figure 7.7). No estate needs an original bottle less than Haut-Brion, Classified First Growth in 1855 and since then served on all royal and presidential tables throughout the world. The Bordeaux bottle has a very distinctive shape. The bottle of Château Haut-Brion respects the tradition, but distinguishes itself with its own original and elegantly distinctive shape evoking the old model of a decanter. It also has an embossed tag of its name on the neck of the bottle.

Figure 7.7   The Haut-Brion bottle
Source: Courtesy of Domaine Clarence Dillon.

In Provence the bottle also has a distinctive shape with its round flanks (see Figure 7.8 on page 166).

What is in the bottle?

A good wine brand is a good wine. When Freixenet launched a new wine, Tapeña, targeting the US market, Tapeña's brand identity, from packaging to flavor profile, was capitalizing on its Spanish heritage. The name is a combination of two Spanish words that have strong cultural connections: *Tapas*, small plates of appetizers traditionally served before

Figure 7.8   The Provence rosé wine bottle
Source: Courtesy of PGA.

meals or as meals, and *peña*, slang for a group of close friends. The goal, said brand manager Erica Odden, 'was to make Spanish wines approach-able for the consumer and to bring the lively, energetic feel of Spain to the U.S. Typically, Spanish wines have been traditional and difficult for consumers to read. Tapeña is the antithesis to that. When you're going for *tapas*, you have your food, your friends and your wine.'[4]

A good quality product easily identifiable by the customer and suggesting a casual lifestyle is likely to be popular. This is certainly the case with the Clarendelle line created by the owners of Château

Haut-Brion. Clarendelle is available in red, white, rosé and sweet. In the presentation of his new wines Robert of Luxembourg, creator of Clarendelle, said: 'We believe that wine lovers are seeking names that they can trust which offer an alternative to existing "new world brands". Clarendelle offers an old world response to a new world creation, Premium Brand Wines. Although the inspiration and style of our wines are firmly anchored in tradition, we are confident that Clarendelle responds to a growing desire of wine lovers who seek wines that are elegant and a joy to drink!' Each of the wines provides a different lifestyle: the elegance and classicism of the red wine is compatible with more formal meals as well as a meal with friends; the freshness and the crispy taste of the white makes it the perfect match for a summer meal or an aperitif. The rosé is delightful with a picnic in the garden or by the river, and the sweet wine will be the perfect substitute or accompaniment for a fruity dessert.

Quality time, casual moments, friendly entertainments – all those are occasions when wine brands provide the answers for new wine drinkers!

The various types of brands

But is a brand just clever packaging marketed by talented people? Or is it the signature of an exceptional quality and international prestige like the Haut-Brion, Margaux or Sissacaïa names?

There are many different kinds of brands in the wine business:

- the luxury brands like the prestigious estates of Haut-Brion or Palmer in Europe, Opus One or Maximus in the United States
- the premium or ultra-premium market with brands like Rosé de Provence or the Black Wine of Cahors based on 'regional branding'
- the mass-market brands: the German Blue Nun in England or the Australian Yellow Tail in the United States.

Luxury wine brands: the organic branding

Haut-Brion, Margaux, Palmer, Sassicaïa, Clos Mogador in the Old World ... Opus One, Maximus in the New World ... These brands are synonymous with luxury, quality, high price, elegance. They are the greatest wines in the world, but they are not only an agricultural product. Their prestige and symbolic status has propelled them to the luxury level. They are not just wine brands, they are *luxury* wine brands.

But because they are an agricultural product as well, they cannot be treated like Calvin Klein jeans. How did they achieve this legendary status? Answer: organic marketing. According to Michael Havens, who founded the Havens Wines Cellars in California, 'Synthetic marketing emphasizes the brand's concept, label and price, followed by the wine; organic marketing focuses on the wine and the region first, followed by concept, label, etc.,' as Havens said to journalist Marvin Collins of *Winesandvines.com* (September 18, 2007).

This concept applies fully to luxury wine brands. Château Haut-Brion and Château Palmer, for example, are wine estates with a long history spanning four centuries. These estates are firmly grounded in a region: Bordeaux, in the Graves area for the first and Margaux for the second. It is the deep knowledge of the soil, the climate and the grapes by the families owning the property and their winemakers, that made this evolution towards greatness possible. The land and the 'Château' (castle or manor house) are part of the history of wine and the history of the country. It is also the story of families who have experienced hardships and joys, successes and failures throughout time. Château Haut-Brion has been owned by only a few families over the centuries. Between Jean de Pontac, who built the castle in 1550, and Joan Dillon, Duchess of Mouchy and her son, Robert de Luxembourg, who are running the estate in the twenty-first century, there have been only two families to have owned Haut-Brion, the Fumels and the Larrieus, if you except the very short ownership of Napoleon's minister Talleyrand. It is the same story with Château Palmer, which was built in the seventeenth century by the de Gascq family, sold to the British General Charles Palmer in 1814 and then to the French bankers, the Pereire brothers, in 1853. Since 1935, it has been owned by three families, the British Sichels, the Dutch Mahler-Besses and the French Bouteillers. Luxury wine brands are a family business.

As Michael Havens said more wittily, it is 'a story of a guy in a place with a grape.' Of course, luxury wine brands are more than just great wines grown in an exceptional place and elegantly bottled. Nowadays it is also a concept. The concept certainly evolved over the years more 'organically' than voluntarily. Each luxury wine brand had to differentiate itself from the others but instead of emphasizing the packaging, they worked on the emotional link they created with their customers. Drinking a glass of Haut-Brion, Palmer or La Romanée Conti is like drinking a little part of European history. I do remember the evening I drank a glass of La Romanée-Conti 1942 during a session of the Académie des Vins Anciens (Academy for Old Wines) founded by François Audouze. It was the winter of 2005, and I was sitting comfortably in the luxurious dining room of the Crillon Hotel in Paris. Seated next to me was Aubert de Villaine, owner of the Domaine de la Romanée-Conti. Of course, the wine was amazing, but even more memorable was the incredibly moving story behind it as told by Villaine who was a child at the time. In 1942, France was occupied by the Nazis; it was a difficult time for winemakers. Most able-bodied men were absent, having been killed, taken prisoner or gone to fight in the 'resistance.' That left only old men, women and children to harvest the grapes and make the wine. As I sat there in the comfortable surroundings of the Crillon dining room sipping the 1942 Romanée-Conti, I realized I was drinking the fruits of their labors, of people most of whom have passed away. I reflected on their pain and suffering, and raised my glass in a silent toast to what they had accomplished.

These are the sort of links and emotions a luxury wine brand can generate in wine lovers. In their *Wine and War* book, Don and Petie Kladstrup tell many of the beautiful stories linked to the wine properties and estates during those tragic years. They even organized a 'wine and war dinner' to celebrate the sixty-first anniversary of D-Day in their Normandy sixteenth-century farm near the landing beaches. On the wine list they offered their guests – all wine lovers and history buffs – 1933 Château Haut-Brion, 1945 Château Montrose, 1942 Clos du Maréchal Pétain (a Burgundy wine) and a 1934 d'Angerville Volnay Premier Cru Champans. Drinking your way through history is the best way to learn it!

Regional brands: a success strategy in the Old World and in the New World

Organic branding, of course, is the privilege of a few luxury wines and not the most common road to fame and success. Most wineries will follow the path of 'synthetic' branding, creating a concept and a label before relying on the place and its history. Some wineries are trying to link the two ideas through regional branding. Traditionally, wine expresses a sense of place, and it is important to educate the consumer in order to make him understand that a wine from France is different from a wine from Spain or California, and that a wine from California is different from a wine from Australia.

Champagne is certainly the most successful case of regional branding. Champagne is a 'terroir,' meaning from a local place in the North-East of France. It is now synonymous with joy, pleasure and celebration. Basing their marketing strategy on this symbolism, the Champagne Houses made a brand out of a local product. It is a guarantee of quality and is now protected as a trademark.

Once the brand 'Champagne' was established, the umbrella brand Champagne relied on the 'individual' brands: Krug, Moët, Roederer, Veuve Clicquot and many others. Those brands are sold worldwide and are a symbol of the French lifestyle.

Following the example of Champagne, some *terroirs* or regions are trying to brand their areas, in order to brand their wines. Every region or area has a specific climate, soils and traditions, and aims to produce a wine quite distinct from their neighbors. The Malbec is a very popular grape produced in many countries. First popular in the Bordeaux area, it is now more connected to Argentina than to Cahors in the South of France, where the grape originated, after its failure in the Bordeaux region. In Cahors, Malbec found its most gorgeous expression because the high and rugged limestone terroir was perfect to fight its weaknesses, a tendency to *coulure* (dying off of the flowers of the vine), rot and downy mildew (mold affecting the vines) as well as a sensitivity to frost.

As we saw in Chapter 4, the Union Interprofessionnelle du Vin de Cahors (Interprofessional Syndicate of Cahors Wine or UIVC) chose a marketing strategy centered on the color of the wine, and labeled it 'Black Wine.' It failed to generate much consumer interest, even if sales went up slightly. As a result, the UIVC is now unfolding the second stage of its strategy: the grape itself, the famous Malbec. Cahors winemakers found a way to overcome its weaknesses and get the best expression from the grape, considered generally to be a 'rustic' and short-lived version. They now create beautifully deep and expressive wines with between 70 percent and 100 percent of Malbec in the bottle.

How is such a change of strategy possible? Because color and gustatory balance are linked. 'Overall, the phenolic balance and the gustatory quality of a wine are related,' wrote Dr. Nicolas Vivas, PhD, from the Enology Laboratory Cesamo. 'We can observe that the Tempranillo grape-variety is at the level of Bordeaux varieties but that the Malbec variety remains at a higher level. This is the logical outcome of the preceding factors: phenolic balance, bright and dark colour, well-maintained fruit aromas and rounded tannins.'[5] These characteristics are linked to the *terroir*.

If the black color and the aromas of the Cahors Malbec are linked to their specific *terroir*, so is the rosé wine from Provence. Considered by historians to be the first wine ever produced, it appeared 2600 years ago in the Mediterranean area including Provence in south-eastern France. The *terroir* is perfect to grow the cinsault, grenache and syrah. Provence wines are blended from different grape varieties selected for their compatibility with the local *terroir*. Each is fermented separately and blended to bring out the best of each style. This is responsible for the unique quality of the wine made, whether it is red, white or rosé. The rosé wine is either classic (dry and fruity), gourmet (richer and sweeter) or fun (light and easily drinkable) and can satisfy the tastes of our new wine drinkers.

Branding an area to brand its wines

Cahors and Provence are not the only regions with branding problems. The Tri-Valley in California is cast in the shadow thrown by its more famous neighbors, Napa and Sonoma. The Tri-Valley area is a triangle-shaped area situated on the east side of San Francisco about 33 miles from the city. It includes three valleys (Amador, Livermore and San Ramon).

With the tagline 'Our roots are showing,' the Tri-Valley area emphasizes its strengths: small town hospitality combined with big-town amenities, home to 38 award-winning wineries, more scenic than Silicon Valley and less commercialized than Napa Valley, an important business hub with less pressure, friendly and laid-back. Quality of life, culture, business and a burgeoning wine industry bring the visitor and the inhabitant back to the cultural roots of the West and the early days of the wine industry in the neighboring Napa. '[T]he Tri-Valley is the real deal,' said Eric Swartz, president and founder of the agency Great Destinations, in charge of the branding of the valley. 'It's just as luxurious, but more affordable; just as elegant, but more casual. It gives visitors a taste of the good life but with greater authenticity and unspoiled vintage charm.'

A brand which spans a number of countries: Invenio

At the opposite end of this strategy of branding a place to brand a wine, companies may create a brand 'which spans a number of countries,' as Tim Corvin, managing director of the agency SiebertHead and creator of the Invenio brand for Carlsberg, stated in his press release.

The beer brewer Carlsberg hired the SiebertHead agency to brand and design its new wine venture, Invenio, which means 'I discover' in Latin, 'therefore providing an association with expert sourcing of wines from around the world,' claimed Corvin without irony. Indeed, the wines have been selected from eight different countries, California, Chile, South Africa, France, Germany, Spain, Italy and Australia and are sold in 15 varieties. Each country is represented with a landscape illustration while the gold scripted logotype conveys premium quality.

The wines have so far only appeared on the UK market but should be available soon in various European countries. Why decide to create a general brand for marketing wines and grapes coming from various and different places? According to Tim Corving, 'often wines from different countries of origin have their own country style, whereas Invenio needed to be "global" not "local." '

This kind of decision is a little difficult to understand when most countries are now recognizing the need for knowing their *terroir* to create the best wines! There is even now a 'Center for Wine Origins' whose first purpose is to teach Americans that for a wine, 'there is no ingredient more important than location. The land, air, water and weather where grapes are grown are what make each wine unique. That's why great names like Port, Champagne and Sherry are more than just types of wine; they're from specific regions in Portugal, France and Spain.'[6]

Australian kangaroos and the global brand: the success of Yellow Tail

Even the famous Yellow Tail – the global brand by definition – is recognized and acknowledged as an Australian brand created by a family, the Casellas, of Italian descent. Yellow Tail exists in ten varieties: Cabernet-Sauvignon, Shiraz, Chardonnay, Pinot Grigio, Pinot Noir, Merlot, Riesling, Shiraz-Cabernet, Shiraz-Grenache, Cabernet-Merlot. It is available in the United States, in Europe (Denmark, Germany, France, United Kingdom, Ireland, Austria, Spain, Belgium, Switzerland, Finland, Italy, Netherlands, Russia), in Asia and in Australia.

The story of Yellow Tail has been told many times. Filippo and Maria Casella arrived in Australia in the 1950s and settled in Yenda, outside Griffith in Northern New South Wales – a region not famous for its wines. Filippo grew grapes and made bulk wines. Life changed when Filippo's son, John, took over and hired John Soutter as general manager. Soutter thought Casella wines had potential to be bottled and marketed to the American market. The lucky break came when Bill Deutsch, who introduced the Beaujolais nouveau Georges Duboeuf into the United States, took some interest in their wines, thinking Australian wines were the new hot category. Soutter sold 20,000 cases from its Carammar Estate to Bill Deutsch. Unfortunately, the wines did not sell at all well, as they looked and tasted too much like any other Australian brands.

John Casella did not become discouraged and decided instead to create a wine with less tannins and acidity. Since he was young himself and thought he could speak for young tastes, he was convinced that tannins and acidity were the elements turning people off many wines. Two other key factors contributed to his success: he put in the bottle a wine he could sell at $10 and then sold it at $6.99; he put the yellow kangaroo on the label. The rest is history. In 2000, he sold 500,000 cases and could not deliver enough wine to the United States. In 2003, he reached five million cases, and, in 2004, Yellow Tail was the number one imported brand in the United States. In 2005, he sold 21 million cases and, in 2006, 25 million. John Casella now owned the biggest Australian winery. In the blinding sun of Yenda stand dozens of steel tanks holding 6 million liters of wine. Yellow Tail represents 8 percent of Australia's production and 15 percent of its total export.

The key factors in the success of Yellow Tail are quite easy to define:

- **The quality of the wine**. Casella wines over-delivered to the consumers for the price being charged.
- **The label**. In 2000, Yellow Tail was the first with a funny moniker. Many brands copied the idea but it was too late.
- **The right place at the right time**. When Casella launched his new brand, the United States was a mature market for an easy-drinking wine with a funny label. It was the beginning of the New Millenium with new consumers.
- **The right people**. Yellow Tail is a global brand but it also has a story. There is a family behind the brand with a moving story which echoes in the American imagination. The Australian dream is very similar to the American dream.

According to Bill Deutsch, there are 5 key factors for the success of a brand he calls the '5 Ps':

1. **Product**. The wine has to be of good quality and be what people want to drink. It also has to be unique.
2. **People**. The people behind the wines are important: do they have a tradition in wine making? Do they love what they do? Do they have a family ready to keep working in the wine business?
3. **Packaging**. It must be original and unique.
4. **Pricing**. It has to be fair for the quality. If the winemaker can afford to over-deliver, so much the better.
5. **Promotion**. It takes a very clever marketing and advertising strategy to capture the consumers' attention while keeping within budget.

Brand recognition

Luxury wine brands, local brands, global brands – they all master the art of marketing their brands in the available markets. But when can the marketer say the brand is recognized?

It depends on what kind of targets were defined at the start. All brands do not satisfy the same needs in the same wine drinkers. Table 7.3 below tries to summarize the answers supplied by the various brands.

Table 7.3   Brand satisfaction

	Luxury	**Tasting**	**Fun**
Satisfied need	Culture	Sensorial	Social
Geographical origin	Medium	Very strong	Weak
Branding	Strong Branding	Weak	Very strong
Taste	Aging Potential	Medium Aging Potential	Fruity and enjoyable

Brand value

The brand is established, the brand is recognized. But is there a financial value to a wine brand? And how is the financial value of a brand calculated?

Evaluating the financial value of a brand is difficult. Indeed, as Nicolas Quille, general manager of Pacific Rim Winemakers stated during the sixteenth Annual Wine Industry Financial Symposium in Napa in

September 2007, a brand is 'an emotional relationship between a consumer and a product that takes the product beyond the commodity level.'
The participants to the Symposium described several important factors
they identified during recent transactions:

- distribution, branding and marketing are important
- vineyard and winery assets are losing ground
- brand-only transactions are increasing
- brand assets include packaging design and art, logos and taglines,
  famous figureheads, production protocols, key contracts, logistic
  contracts
- suppliers, distributors
- inventory levels
- profit margins
- employment
- trademark and intellectual properties.

Of course, no figures were disclosed during the symposium, but it was
made clear that sometimes brands are more valuable than the land
because of the human and emotional value of the brand. 'It is not just
about dollars,' stated Pat DeLong, CFO of Leucadia Cellars. 'It depends
how important brand integrity is to the seller.'

Conclusion

From the vineyard to the glass, wine is a cultural, emotional and commercial product. It has a value – real and virtual. All its contradictions
and complexities worldwide make it a controversial subject. Branding or
not branding? Nobody knows the answer – except maybe the wine
drinker who will buy your wine, proving you right, or who will not buy
your wine, proving you wrong.

But right or wrong does not matter. Before being a commercial
endeavor, wine is about taste, pleasure, people and places. It is about
tradition, emotion, history – past and present. Indeed, the contemporary
brands might become the wines of our children and grandchildren. They
will tell the next generations what our life was about.

Notes

1 Portrait of a man as a traditional consumer

1. Cited by D. and P. Kladstrup, *Champagne*, p. 93.
2. Ibid., p. 95.
3. Ibid., p. 112.
4. Ibid., p. 115.
5. Ibid., p. 206.
6. Ibid.
7. Cited by Barbara Holland, *The Joy of Drinking*, p. 57.
8. Cited ibid., p. 59.
9. Ibid., p. 63.
10. From ibid., p. 64.
11. C. Malanga, 'He Held Good Taste to Be Self-Evident', City-journal.org, August 31, 2007.
12. Ibid.
13. From Holland, *The Joy of Drinking*, p. 74.
14. From Dr. James McWilliams, *A Revolution In Eating: How the Quest for Food Shaped America* (April 2005).
15. From the title of an article by Paul Hart, 'Chicago, Big Shoulders, Open Minds, Sharp Palates', in *The World of Fine Wines*, issue 16, 2007, pp. 130–7. This section is inspired by his article.
16. Ibid., p. 131.
17. My thanks to Randy for doing the maths!
18. Cited by Pieter Eijkhoff, in *Wine in China: Its History and Contemporary Developments*, MS Netherlands Wine Guild, 2000, p. 33.
19. Ibid., pp. 101–2.
20. Inspired from http://en.wikipedia.org/wiki/Russian_cuisine.

2 Values and trends of the new consumers

1. Patrick Dixon, *Futurewise*, Profile Book, London, 2007, p. xvi.
2. Ibid., p. xvii.
3. Ibid., p. 1.
4. Ibid., pp. 14–15.
5. www.pr.com, 'Free Wiki Wine Rating Site Let's Visitors Find the Best Wines in Their Area', press release of WineApe.com.
6. Ibid.

 7. P. Dixon, *Futurewise*, p. 157.
 8. Hispanicprnews.com, May 18, 2004.
 9. Ibid.
10. Interview in Paris with Nathalie Vranken, September 2007.
11. From the site http://www.libation-unlimited.com/i-87-champagne-pommery-pop.aspx, presentation of the POP Champagne.
12. Pamela N. Danziger, *Why People Buy Things They Don't Need*, p. 24.
13. P. Dixon, *Futurewise*, p. 180.
14. Ibid., p. 190.
15. Ibid., p. 196.
16. Ibid., p. 241.
17. http://blanc-de-noir.blogspot.com/2007/05/think-pink-ros-wine-tasting-aids-breast.html, May 27, 2007.
18. http://www.marininstitute.org/marin/sutter_home.htm

3 Birth of the new wine consumer

 1. Amrit Dhillon, 'Blank looks go as India develops thirst for wine', *Telegraph.co.uk*, May 21, 2007.
 2. The studies we are mostly referring to are: the 2005 Wine Intelligence study of UK drinkers; the 2006 Constellation Wines study of US wine drinkers; the 2007 Vinexpo study of European wine drinkers; and the 2005 Vinagora study of French drinkers. Unfortunately, I was unable to access any Japanese study in English.

4 Traditional marketing versus web marketing

 1. From Jancis Robinson's *Guide to Wine Grapes*.
 2. Harvey Posert and Paul Franson, *Spinning the Bottle*, p. 152.
 3. Ibid., p. 153.
 4. Ibid., p. 154.
 5. George Raine, Wine Market Council.
 6. http://www.packagingeurope.com/NewsDetails.aspx?nNewsID=15031, *Silver Palm Cabernet Sauvignon Proves 'Beauty Is In the Details'*, Sept. 3, 2007.
 7. http://www.château-palmer.com/en82, portrait of Daniel Paquette.
 8. http://www.wineinacan.com/about_us
 9. http://www.wineinacan.com/our_range
10. http://www.wineinacan.com/vinsafe
11. Article by Linda Murphy, *San Francisco Chronicle*, March 8, 2007.
12. D. Solomon, 'Ernest and Julio and Me', in *Spinning the Bottle*, pp. 193–7.
13. From 'Gina Gallo has winemaking in her blood', by Madelyn Miller, TheTravelLadyMagazine.com.
14. Interview with Gerri-Lynn Becker, Marketing Director of the California Wine Club.
15. This story is narrated by Don and Petie Kladstrup in, 'In Vino Caritas: Drinking Well and Doing Good', *The World of Fine Wines*, pp. 88–93.

5 Pouring wines in new ways: marketing on Web 1.0

1. Interview with Tom Cannavan, April 16, 2007.
2. From the web site of the Connoisseur Club.
3. The calculation formula is: price x number of impressions/clicks.
4. Press Kit of *E-Performance Barometer*, presented at Vinexpo on June 20, 2007, p. 4.
5. Ibid., p. 5.
6. Ibid., p. 15.
7. Brandchannel, Brad Cook, wine.com by eVineyards, September 2, 2002.
8. Mark Del Franco, *Wine.com Launches Print Book*, online article, November 13, 2002.
9. From *San Francisco Business Times*, May 4, 2005.

6 Web 2.0 and the new millennium: innovative ways for new trends

1. Karen Lee, 'Netnographic investigation of online communities: Implications for Online Data Collections, Analysis and Advertising management', Prepared for Quantitative Methods in Advertising and Brand Communication, ADV 391K, at the University of Texas, April 22, 2004.
2. As we are now talking about bobos and Millennials!
3. Darryl Roberts, *The Autobiography of Wine X, Or Explaining Rain ... to People Who Don't Know What Water Is*, WineX website, 2003.
4. Cited by Alexandre Chomley, in /Influencia Magazine/, October 11, 2007.

7 Wine and branding

1. http://wineanorak.com, blog, 'The two cultures', November 2002.
2. brandchannel.com
3. In his blog, wineanorak.com, *The Two Cultures*, November 2002.
4. Cited in winebusiness.com – April 2, 2007, *Freixenet Launches New Spanish Brand*, by Mary-Colleen Tinney.
5. From the press kit of Union Interprofessionnelle des Vins de Cahors (UIVC), Cahors, Legendary Malbec.
6. http://www.wineorigins.com/, home page, Mission Statement.

Bibliography

Books and articles

Chris Anerson, *The Long Tail: How Endless Choice is Creating Unlimited Demand*, Random House Books, London, 2006.

Monisha Bharadwaj, *Saveurs des Indes*, Marabout, Côté Cuisine, 1996.

Warren Belasco, *Meals to Come: A History of the Future of Food* (California Studies in Food and Culture 16), University of California Press. Berkeley and Los Angeles, 2006.

Maurice Bensoussan, *Le Ketchup et le Gratin, Histoire(s) parallèle(s) des habitudes alimentaires françaises et américaines*, Éditions Assouline, Paris, 1999.

Claude Boutineau, with Jean-Noël Kapferer, *Le dirigeant et la planète consommateurs. Les réalités du marketing mondial*, Village Mondial, HEC, 2005.

Asa Briggs, *Haut-Brion*, Faber & Faber, London, 1994.

Martin Bruegel and Bruno Laurious (dir.), *Histoire et identités alimentaires en Europe*, Hachette Littérature, Paris, 2002.

Steven Charters, *Wine and Society: The Cultural and Social Context of a Drink*, 2006.

Vincent Chenille, *Le plaisir gastronomique au cinéma, foreword by Jean-Luc DOUIN*, ed. Jean-Paul Rocher, Éditions Mutine, Paris, 2004.

Linda Civitello, *Cuisine and Culture: A History of Food and People*, John Wiley & Sons, New York, 2007.

David Darlington, *Wine & Spirits* (25th Anniversary Issue, Summer 2007).

Joan Dejean, *The Essence of Style: How the French Invented High Fashion, Fine Food, Chic Cafés, Style, Sophistication, and Glamour*, Free Press, New York, 2005.

Pamela N. Danziger, *Why People Buy Things They Don't Need: Understanding and Predicting Consumer Behaviour*, Dearborn, Chicago, 2004.

Patrick Dixon, *Futurewise – Six Faces of Global*, HarperCollins, London, 3rd edn, 2004.

Pieter Eijkhoff, *Wine in China: Its History and Contemporary Developments*, MS Netherlands Wine Guild, 2000.

Jean-Louis Flandrin and Jane Cobbi, *Tables d'hier, Tables d'ailleurs*, Édition Odile Jacob, Paris, 1999.

Jean-Louis Flandrin and Massimo Montanari (dir.), *Histoire de l'alimentation*, Fayard, Paris, 1996.

Gilles Fumey and Olivier Etcheverria, *Atlas Mondial des cuisines et gastronomies, Une géographie gourmande*, Éditions Autrement, Paris, 2004.

Gilbert Garrier, *Histoire sociale et culturelle du vin*, Bordas, Coll. Cultures, 1996.

Barry Glasner, *The Gospel of Food: Everything you Think you Know About Food Is Wrong*, Ecco/HarperCollins, London, 2007.

Thomas Gwinner and Zhenzuan Zhang, *Les Grandes traditions culinaires de la Chine de L'Ouest*, Time-Life, Amsterdam, n.d.

John Hailman, *Thomas Jefferson on Wine*, University Press of Mississipi., Jackson, 2007.

Barbara Holland, *The Joy of Drinking*, 2007, Bloomsbury, London.

Mack Holt, *Alcohol: A Social and Cultural History*, Berg, Oxford, 2006.

Araki Joh, Shinobu Kaitani and Ken-Ichi Hori, *Sommelier*, Édition Glénat, Paris, 2006, vols 1 and 2.

Don and Petie Kladstrup, *Wine and War, The French, the Nazis and the Battle for France's Greatest Treasure*, Broadway Books, Portland: OR, 2001.

Don and Petie Kladstrup, *Champagne, How the World's Most Glamorous Wine Triumphed over War and Hard Times*, HarperCollins, London, 2005.

Don and Petie Kladstrup, 'In Vino Caritas: Drinking Well and Doing Good', published in *The World of Fine Wines* (Issue 17, 2007).

Georges Lewi, *Memento Pratique du Branding*, Village, New York, 2006.

Paul Lukacs, *American Vintage: The Rise of American Wine*, W.W. Norton, New York, 2000.

Mille et une bouches. Cuisines et identités culturelles, dirigé par Sophie Bessis, Série Mutations/mangeurs n° 154, Editions Autrement, 1995.

James McWilliams, *A Revolution In Eating: How the Quest for Food Shaped America*, Columbia University Press, New York, 2005.

Anjali Mendes, *La cuisine indienne*, Albin Michel, Paris, 2002.

Etienne Montaigne, Jean-Pierre Couderc, François d'Hauteville and Hervé Hanin (dir), *Bacchus 2006, Enjeux, stratégies et pratiques dans la filière vitivinicole*, Dunod, 2005.

Pierre Mora and Yohan Castaing, *Bonnes pratiques en marketing du vin, 20 études de cas de vins du monde*, Dunod, 2005.

Didier Nourrisson, *Le buveur du XIXe siècle*, Albin Michel, Paris, 1990.

Thomas Pinney, *A History of Wine in America: From Prohibition to the Present*, University of California Press, 2005.

Harvey Posert and Paul Franson, *Spinning the Bottle. Case Histories, Tactics and Stories of Wine Public Relations*, HPPR Press, St. Helena, CA, 2004.

Jancis Robinson, *Guide to Wine Grapes, A Unique A-Z Reference to Grape Varieties and the Wines They Produce*, Oxford University Press, 1996.

Anthony Rowley and Jean-Claude Ribaut, *Le Vin. Une histoire de goût*, Découvertes Gallimard, Paris, 2003.

Céline Simonnet-Toussaint, *Le Vin sur le Divan*. Feret, Bourdeaux, 2006.

Paul Wagner, Janeen Olsen and Liz Thach, *Wine Marketing and Sales: Success Strategies for A Saturated Market*, The Wine Appreciation Guild, San Francisco, 2007.

Thomas M. Wilson, (dir.), 'Food, Drink and Identity in Europe', *European Studies*, 2006.

Resources on line

www.ireb.com/publications/focus/IREB%20Focus%20n6.pdf: Revue *Focus, Alcoologie*, Institut de Recherches Scientifiques sur les Boissons, *La consommation d'alcool en Europe, Chiffres et déchiffrages, Alcohol consumption in Europe, Deciphering the Figures*. Including interviews with:

   Patrick Aigrain (ONIVINS, National Interprofessional Office for Wine – France).
   Björn Hibell (CAN, Swedish Council for Information on Alcohol and other Drugs), n°6, 2003. (bilingual).

http://sommelier-india.com: the only blog, coupled with a paper magazine, on the Indian wine industry.

http://septimanie-export.com: information on the export of wines in the world (in French).

http://www.frenchentree.com/france-lot-quercy-cahors-wine/DisplayArticle.asp?ID9394: information on Quercy area and Cahors black wine (in English).

http://vinesandwines.com: *Marketing Matters*, *Building Loyalty with Customer Blending*, March 1, 2007, by Tina Caputo.

http://sfchronicle.com: Ernest Gallo obituary, by Linda Murphy, March 8, 2007.

Index